IN THE FOOTSTEPS OF

ROBERT BRUCE

Glencoe. Bruce had to march through mountainous terrain in 1307 to defeat his enemies in northern Scotland.

IN THE FOOTSTEPS OF

ROBERT BRUCE

IN SCOTLAND, NORTHERN ENGLAND AND IRELAND

ALAN YOUNG & MICHAEL J. STEAD

Front cover: Swaledale and Robert Bruce's statue, Stirling Castle.

Back cover: Guisborough Priory, Yorkshire.

Front endpapers: Innis Chonnel Castle.

Back endpapers: Drumochter Pass.

First published in 1999
This edition published in 2010

The History Press
The Mill, Brimscombe Port
Stroud, Gloucestershire, GL5 2QG
www.thehistorypress.co.uk

British Library Cataloguing in Publication Data.
A catalogue record for this book is available from the British Library.

ISBN 978 0 7524 5642 3

Typesetting and origination by The History Press
Printed in India by Nutech Print Services
Manufacturing managed by Jellyfish Print Solutions Ltd

CONTENTS

Rievaulx Abbey. The Scottish army came close to surprising and capturing Edward II here in 1322. The English King was fortunate to escape – as he had been at Bannockburn in 1314.

PREFACE

Robert Bruce has remained a potent symbol of Scottish nationalism since he won that status, heroically, at the Battle of Bannockburn in 1314. That achievement lives on with the adoption of 'Flower of Scotland' as an unofficial national anthem. Yet recent research shows that the long-established tradition of Robert Bruce as 'saviour and champion' of Scotland forms only one element of his story. Behind the legend is a more complex and, in many ways, more fascinating picture of a man who overcame great odds to fulfil his family's long-held desire for political, indeed dynastic, power. The means of achieving this end involved Bruce in the murky world of power politics, which was rife with ambition, intrigue, opportunism and even murder. This perspective does not sit easily alongside the more romantic and heroic image of Bruce so vigorously asserted by Scottish patriotic writings of the fourteenth and fifteenth centuries. It is, nevertheless, part of the real world of Robert Bruce.

This book will examine both sides of Bruce's life and career. It will explore both the harsh reality of political life at the end of the thirteenth and the beginning of the fourteenth centuries and the popular legend of Bruce, the patriot hero. In order to understand these components, Robert Bruce will first be placed in the context of his family and its developing aspirations during the twelfth and thirteenth centuries. The difficulties faced by Robert Bruce in fulfilling the family's ultimate ambition – dynastic power in Sco tland – will be traced by detailing the nature of late thirteenth-century Scottish politics and Anglo-Scottish relations. Until Robert Bruce's coup of 1306, the Bruces, though powerful and competitive, were in practice excluded from power in Scotland by an even more mighty and well-established governing clique. In this context, a Scottish civil war raged alongside an Anglo-Scottish war between 1306 and 1314. The Battle of Bannockburn was probably just as significant in the context of the civil war as it was for the Anglo-Scottish war. Victory here formed an important part of Robert Bruce's transformation from Scottish rebel to patriot hero and accepted leader of the new Scottish political establishment.

The narrative of Bruce's acquisition of the leadership of the Scottish political community is accompanied by illuminating contemporary commentaries. This book also aims to illustrate the varied settings and sites that recur in the Bruce story. Unlike other heroes of British history such as King Arthur and Robin Hood, the itinerary of Robert Bruce can, to a large extent, still be traced today. Not all sites visited by Bruce still exist – his military tactics ensured that many enemy castles were systematically destroyed after capture – but the landscape in which Bruce operated still conjures up powerful images of his presence. These places range from those associated with the Bruce family's early roots in north Yorkshire, south Durham and Cumberland to, particularly, the family's early bases in southwest Scotland, where Robert Bruce himself was born. Also featured are those areas controlled by the Bruces' enemies in northern Scotland – the Highlands, the Great Glen, Argyll and north-eastern Scotland. The images of these landscapes underline the domination of key land and water routes in northern Scotland by families such as the Comyns, Macdougalls and Morays – they also emphasise the task Bruce faced if he was to consolidate his coup of 1306. Following Bannockburn, Robert Bruce was free to extend his sphere of influence beyond Scotland in order to force recognition of his status as Scottish king as well as the independence of the Scottish kingdom. Sweeping raids affected most areas in northern England, both in the west and east, and key northern cities such as Carlisle, Durham and even York were under constant threat as Bruce's forces reached deep into Yorkshire. The opening of a new war front in Ireland also put extra pressure on the English monarchy. All of the images in this book chart Robert Bruce's career in Scotland, Ireland and across northern England too, areas that keenly felt his influence.

ACKNOWLEDGEMENTS

Any study of Robert Bruce must acknowledge the immense contribution made by the research and writing of Professor G.W.S. Barrow and Professor A.A.M. Duncan and to the recent work of Dr C. McNamee. Professor Barrow's guidance and advice over many years has been an inspiration and we are most grateful for his generosity in sharing his great knowledge of Scottish history and landscape. This book has greatly benefited from his helpful suggestions and in commenting on the book's final draft he has saved us from making a number of mistakes. The errors that remain are entirely our own responsibility, as are the opinions contained in the book.

A number of individuals and institutions have contributed greatly to the completion of this work. In particular, we would like to give special thanks to Historic Scotland for kindly allowing us to photograph sites in their care and to Mr Joseph White (Historic Scotland) for help in sourcing photographs. Research on Bruce seals was greatly facilitated by the assistance of Mrs G.C.W. Roads, Lyon Clerk and Keeper of the Records at the Court of the Lord Lyon. Thanks are also due to the Scottish Record Office for assistance with document research and to the National Monuments Record of Scotland (RCAHMS).

We are most grateful to Joanne Ripley for the speedy and efficient way in which the final draft was put on disk. Thanks are also due to Jaqueline Mitchell and Alison Flowers of Sutton Publishing for both supporting this project and helping it efficiently along its way, and also to Jo de Vries and Siubhan Macdonald at The History Press. Finally, we must thank Diane Olsen for bringing together a medieval historian and a landscape photographer to discuss potential co-operative ventures. Hopefully, this will be the first of many.

Alan Young
Michael J. Stead

The Bruce Tomb, St Hilda's Church, Hartlepool.

ROBERT BRUCE, HERO KING

'**O**n 7 June 1329 died Robert Bruce, of goodly memory, the illustrious king of Scots, at Cardross [on the Clyde] in the twenty-fourth year of his reign. He was, beyond all living men of his day, a valiant knight.' These are the words of John of Fordun who wrote *The Chronicle of the Scottish Nation* in the 1380s and whose work forms the main strand in the standard narrative account of Scottish medieval history. Shortly before, in 1375, John Barbour wrote *The Bruce*, the most comprehensive life of a medieval king in the west, in the form of an epic poem with Robert Bruce as the chivalric hero. These two works have very firmly laid the foundation for the great Scottish tradition that has remained strong for over six hundred years – that of Robert Bruce as hero king, champion of Scottish nationalism against English imperialism.

Proof of the special, indeed unique, place of Robert Bruce in Scottish history is not only provided by literature. Bruce's remains, themselves, have been treated with the reverence usually accorded to a saint. Bruce's body was buried in Dunfermline Abbey, where it was found encased in lead almost five hundred years later. The discovery beneath the middle of the choir was made during alterations to the church in 1819. A cast of Bruce's skull was taken at the time of the excavation and contemporary reports emphasise the extreme care taken with the precious remains.

The report on the find noted that the skeleton was of a man between 5 ft 11 in and 6 ft tall. Conclusive proof that the skeleton

Bruce's grave, Dunfermline Abbey. Since Malcolm Canmore's time, the abbey had replaced Iona as the sepulchre of Scottish kings. Bruce's remains, found in 1818, were wrapped in a cloth-of-gold shroud.

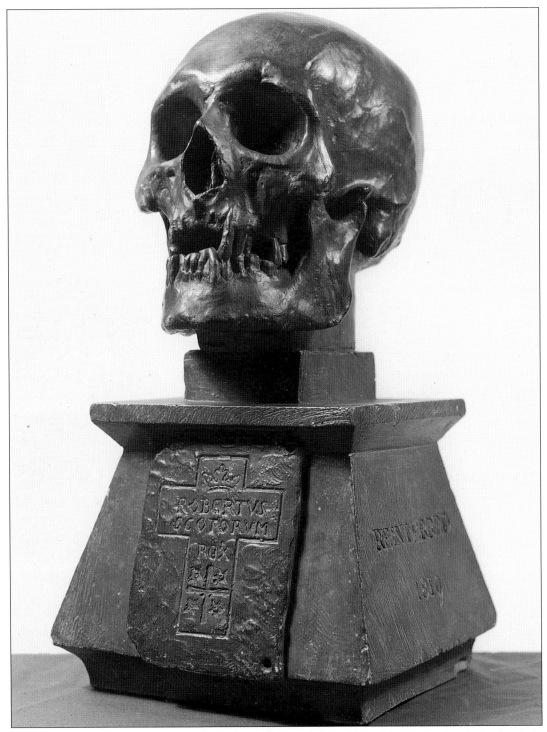

The cast of Robert Bruce's skull. Robert Bruce's body was discovered encased in lead during alterations to the church at Dunfermline Abbey in 1819; a cast of the skull was taken at that time. Courtesy of the Scottish National Portrait Gallery.

was that of Robert Bruce lay in the fact that the breastbone had been sawn apart to allow the heart to be removed. It is known that Bruce, on his deathbed, had asked that his heart should be taken from his body and, after embalming, carried to the crusades. Thus he would, after death, be able to fulfil his ambition of going on crusade and visiting the Holy Sepulchre. In 1330, a year after Robert Bruce's death, James Douglas, a close friend and ally, journeyed to Spain with Bruce's heart. King Alfonso XI of Castile and León was, at the time, campaigning against the Moors of Granada and James Douglas led a division of the Christian army at the Battle of Tebas de Ardales on 30 March 1330. He bore the heart of Robert Bruce into the battle thus fulfilling Bruce's wish to fight against the infidel. Unfortunately, Douglas was cut off and killed by the Moors in the battle and both his bones and Bruce's heart were, subsequently, returned to Scotland for burial. The heart of Robert Bruce was finally buried at Melrose Abbey in accordance with Bruce's wishes. In a sense, Bruce was following family tradition in wishing to be associated with the crusades. His grandfather had gone to the Holy Land in 1270. It is also possible, however, that guilt over his involvement in the mortal, not to say sacrilegious, wounding of his chief rival, John Comyn, Lord of Badenoch, in the Greyfriars Church at Dumfries on 10 February 1306, may have motivated a late attempt to save his soul.

Both Bruce's skeleton and his heart have been the subject of much recent attention. In 1996 a terracotta likeness of Bruce's face was unveiled at the Scottish National Portrait Gallery (Edinburgh) to go alongside the cast of Bruce's skull on which the reconstruction was based. As for Bruce's heart, it lay buried at Melrose Abbey until the 1920s when archaeologists discovered the lead conical container and returned it in a modern casket. Unfortunately, the burial spot was not marked. This casket was refound in 1996, opened by archaeologists from Historic Scotland and returned in June 1998, this time with a stone to mark the heart's reburial for the third time in its history.

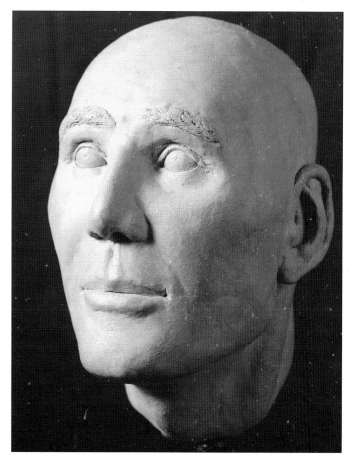

The terracotta likeness of Robert Bruce's head. Forensic work on the skull cast at Newcastle Dental Hospital revealed Bruce's war wounds – he survived blows to the head, left eye and front teeth. Courtesy of the Scottish National Portrait Gallery.

ROBERT BRUCE, PATRIOT HERO

The Robert Bruce Statue, Bannockburn. Pilkington Jackson's bronze statue dedicated to Robert Bruce was modelled on the equestrian representation on the king's Second Great Seal.

The image of Robert Bruce as patriot hero was firmly laid by Scottish writers of the fourteenth and fifteenth centuries. The influential John of Fordun, who wrote *The Chronicle of the Scots Nation* in the 1380s, described how 'God in His mercy . . . raised up a saviour and a champion unto them . . . Robert Bruce. The man . . . underwent the countless and unbearable toils of the heat of the day . . . for the sake of freeing his brethren'. Walter Bower's *Scotichronicon* was written in a similar tone in about 1440: 'whoever has learned to recount his [Robert Bruce's] individual conflicts and particular triumphs . . . will find, I think, that he

Reverse of the Second Great Seal of Robert I. The king is shown on horseback in chain mail with crowned helmet.
By permission of the Court of the Lord Lyon.

Obverse of the Second Great Seal of Robert I. This seal was in use from 1316 and was modelled on the seal of Louis X of France. The king is seen on his throne but the carved gothic armchair throne is abandoned and the king is posed more naturally. By permission of the Court of the Lord Lyon.

will judge none in the regions of the world to be his equals in his own times in the art of fighting and in physical strength'. John Barbour's biography, *The Bruce*, written in 1375, chronicled Bruce's achievement in great detail, portraying Bruce as the chivalric hero of an epic poem: 'King Robert Bruce who was brave in heart and hand'. Such works developed the exalted view of Robert Bruce already being promoted through government propaganda from 1309 onwards. It is this view that is represented in visual form through the King's seals and statues.

Guisborough Priory, the Bruce family's main religious base before the Scottish wars, did not escape the warfare when Robert Bruce's raids reached down into Yorkshire.

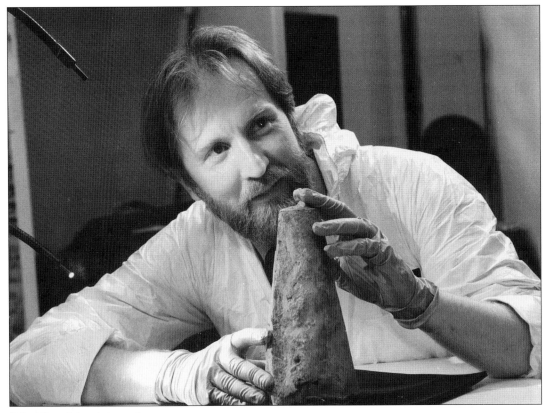

Robert Bruce's heart. A member of the Historic Scotland staff examines the casket holding the mummified heart of Bruce rediscovered at Melrose Abbey in 1996 and subsequently reburied in June 1998. Crown Copyright: Reproduced Permission of Historic Scotland.

Dunfermline and Melrose abbeys are places naturally held in reverence in the history of Robert Bruce. However, the place most associated with Robert Bruce is Bannockburn, the site of Bruce's famous victory over the English forces of Edward II in 1314. Bannockburn and Bruce's triumph are celebrated in the contemporary, and popular, national anthem 'Flower of Scotland'. In physical form the 650th anniversary of Bannockburn was commemorated in 1964 by the magnificent Pilkington Jackson statue of Bruce. Bannockburn is naturally acknowledged as the site of the climax of Robert Bruce's career and deserves special attention but it tends to overshadow many other locations and settings that played a part in the career of a remarkable man.

Behind the rather one-dimensional legend of Bruce as the hero of Scottish nationalism is a more complex, and perhaps more fascinating, picture. Robert Bruce was a man who overcame great odds (often much underplayed) to win power for himself in Scotland and fulfil his family's long-held ambition to exert political influence in Scotland. It was after this that he had to fight off the English forces in order to retain that power.

Robert Bruce must first of all be seen in the context of his family and their aspirations. The Bruce family made its first mark in Britain in the early years of the twelfth century, largely as a result of the family's close relationship with Henry I, the youngest son of William the Conqueror, and King of England from 1100 to 1135. The first Robert Bruce came from Brix in the Cotentin. The Bruce family were rewarded for their support of Henry I in his conquest of Normandy, an acquisition ultimately confirmed at the Battle of Tinchebrai (1106). They received an extensive but compact lordship in North Yorkshire, part of it by 1103 and the rest by 1110. The first Robert Bruce served Henry I as justice, i.e. chief royal agent, in the north of England at a time when Norman political and administrative authority in the north was still insecure and Yorkshire was a border zone. The Bruces were fortunate, however, to have not one but two royal patrons. The King of Scots, David I (1124–53) had also been a close friend of Henry I, and in 1124 granted Robert Bruce Annandale and its castles in south-west Scotland. Bruce, by his death in 1142, had also acquired land north of the Tees, the fief of Hartness including the manor of Hart and the important port of Hartlepool. He was the founder of the Scottish and Yorkshire branches of the Bruce family.

The 'caput' or head of Bruce's North Yorkshire lands was Skelton, although another important base was Danby. The present Skelton Castle essentially dates from about 1800 but there was a Bruce castle there in

The grave of Robert Bruce at Melrose Abbey. Robert Bruce made a deathbed wish for his heart to be buried here after it was taken on Crusade by James Douglas.

Guisborough Priory, Yorkshire. From its foundation in 1119 by Robert de Brus of Skelton to the burial of King Robert's grandfather in 1295, Guisborough was the Bruces' major religious base. Ironically, it suffered from Robert Bruce's raids.

Melrose Abbey. One of the finest Cistercian ruins in Britain, the abbey was founded in 1136 from Rievaulx. The earliest buildings have largely been destroyed as a result of the harsh treatment by the armies of Edward I and II.

the twelfth century. There is, however, no visible evidence of this except the site of a moat 240 ft wide enclosing a diamond-shaped area of 5½ acres. A rather more significant physical symbol of this early Bruce lordship is Guisborough Priory, founded by Robert Bruce in about 1119 for Augustinian canons. It was a rich foundation, the first religious centre for the Bruces in Britain. As such it remained important to the Bruces of both Annandale and Yorkshire throughout the twelfth and thirteenth centuries. It was natural for the first Robert Bruce, the founder, to be buried there in 1142. What is more remarkable is that over 150 years later, Robert Bruce, the future King's grandfather, was buried there in 1295 on the eve of the Scottish wars, his body being brought from Annandale, his main base at that time. According to the *Chronicle of Lanercost*: 'The lord Robert de Brus, a noble baron of England as well as of Scotland, heir of Annandale, departed from this world, aged and full of days . . . He rests with his ancestors at Gisburne [Guisborough] but it was in Annan that he yielded up his spirit to the angels, the chief town of that district'. The town of Guisborough must have grown up at the very gates of the priory. In 1263, Henry III granted it a weekly market, an important contribution to the town's economic development. In 1289, a fire destroyed the original church at Guisborough Priory so the present remains are later than this date. The only surviving buildings of that fire are to the west, the octagonal priory dovecote and gatehouse from about 1200. Testament to the Bruces' long-established influence in Guisborough is given by the remarkable sixteenth-century Bruce cenotaph in the parish church of St Nicholas at Guisborough. The cenotaph was originally in the priory immediately south of the parish church.

The early Bruces made a similar impact on the development of Hartlepool as a town and port. Hartlepool was part of the fief of Hartness (north of the Tees), which was in the possession of the first Robert Bruce by his death in 1142; it is uncertain whether this came to him through Henry I of England or David I of Scotland, who exercised effective control north of the Tees in the early 1140s. In the time of King John

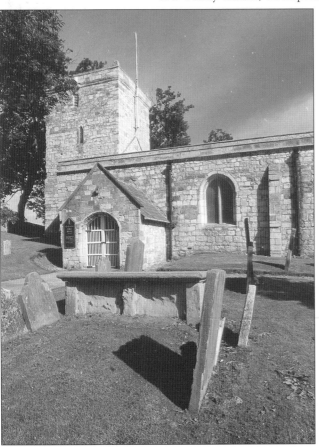

Hart Church, Co. Durham, was part of the Bruce fief of Hartness, north of the Tees, and was granted to Guisborough Priory in the mid-twelfth century.

The Bruce Tomb, St Hilda's Church, Hartlepool. The worn male effigy on the weathered altar tomb is thought to be a member of the Bruce family. Bruce associations with Hartlepool did not prevent Scottish raids.

(1199–1216), William Bruce, third Bruce Lord of Annandale, helped the burgesses of Hartlepool – as a town Hartlepool certainly existed by the mid-twelfth century – to buy their market and fair charter from the English King. Visible evidence of the Bruces' effect on Hartlepool can be detected in the impressive remains of the parish church of St Hilda, close to the tip of the peninsula on which Hartlepool originated. The unusual size, richness and quality of this thirteenth-century church – its large, spacious nave, impressive chancel arch and the west bay of the chancel – suggest that the church may have been built by the Bruces as a family burial place. The large, weathered altar tomb of Frosterley marble incorporates a worn male effigy thought to be a member of the Bruce family.

In south-west Scotland, an area that became the heartland of the Scottish Bruces, the first Robert Bruce had acquired the lands of Annandale in 1124 as a military fief. The younger son of this Robert, another Robert, was to develop this Scottish branch of the Bruce family. David I was seeking to use the Bruces to define royal authority in the south-west, a notoriously separatist area. Thus the Bruces were being employed as a frontier family by two kings and two kingdoms in the early twelfth century. The military fief of Annandale was centred on the two castles of Annan and Lochmaben. The original head or 'caput' of

Overleaf:
Lochmaben, a chief stronghold of the Bruces of Annandale. Only a motte (on a golf course south-west of the town) remains of the earliest site, which was replaced by a late thirteenth-century stone castle at the south end of Castle Loch.

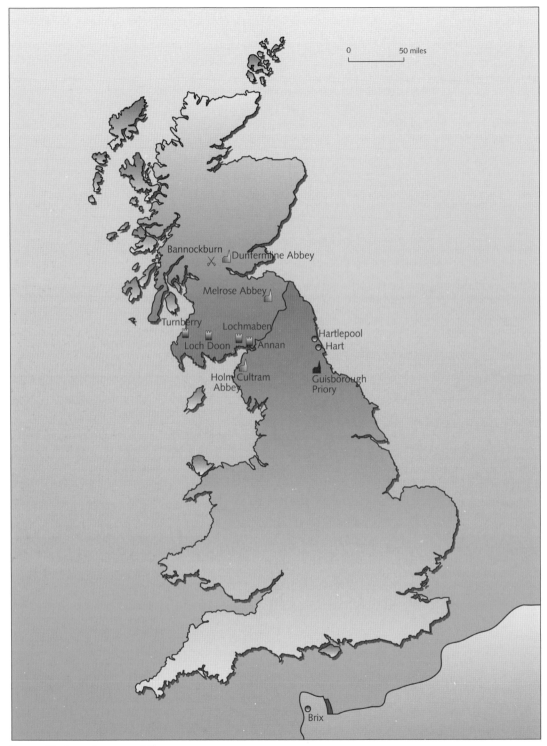

0   50 miles

Bannockburn   Dunfermline Abbey

Melrose Abbey

Turnberry   Lochmaben   Hartlepool
Loch Doon   Annan   Hart

Holm Cultram   Guisborough
Abbey   Priory

Brix

Places with strong Bruce associations.

these Scottish lands was Annan where the burgh grew up by the side of a defended river crossing. However, in about 1200 the waters of the River Annan washed away part of Annan Castle forcing the Bruces to make their chief residence at Lochmaben. The fate of Annan is normally associated with the curse laid on it by the great Irish reformer and saint, St Malachy, who stayed at Annan in about 1140 with Robert Bruce II of Annandale. At St Malachy's behest, Robert promised to pardon a thief but broke his promise and hanged him instead. To the cynical modern mind, the subsequent destruction of Annan Castle by flood would seem little more than coincidence. However, the curse of St Malachy, a formidable personality by all accounts, was taken seriously by generations of Bruces. In 1272, Robert Bruce, the future King's grandfather, returning from crusade made a special visit to the famous Cistercian abbey at Clairvaux where St Malachy was buried. He prayed at his tomb and gave a gift of land in Annandale to pay for lights to burn for ever at St Malachy's shrine. In the early thirteenth century, Bruce patronage of Melrose Abbey, perhaps the most important Cistercian house in Scotland, may also be connected with the curse of St Malachy. Melrose Abbey was specifically named by the future King Robert Bruce as the burial place for his heart.

Already by the 1150s the Bruces seem to have been developing a motte and bailey castle at Lochmaben. (This first castle site now serves as the fourteenth tee on the golf course south-west of the town.) The summit of the mound (or motte) is very large, oval in plan and surrounded by a ditch. This early castle was superseded by the stone castle, which occupies a promontory at the southern end of Castle Loch. The building work was probably undertaken in the second half of the thirteenth century, by which time the Bruces had begun to accumulate significant landed wealth in both England and Scotland. A notable feature of the stone castle at Lochmaben is a canal over 6 ft wide that lies in front of the south curtain wall. When the level of the loch was higher, boats would have been able to gain access to the castle via the canal. The castle at Lochmaben, where some curtain walls survive to their original height, was to play a key role in the Anglo-Scottish wars.

St Hilda's Church, Hartlepool. The size and quality of this thirteenth-century church is testimony to Bruce patronage and the prosperity of the medieval port of Hartlepool.

Maiden's Bay, Turnberry. Little now remains of Turnberry Castle, chief castle of the Bruce Earls of Carrick and dismantled on Bruce's orders in 1310. The site is situated close to Turnberry Bay and Maiden's Bay.

The increasing landed wealth of the Bruces by the mid-thirteenth century has already been noted. It came about through good marriages – particularly significant is the marriage of Robert, fourth Lord of Annandale (d. *c*. 1230) to Isabel, second daughter of David, Earl of Huntingdon. This brought the Bruces of Annandale, through inheritance, lands in the eastern Midlands of England and the important lands of Garioch in Aberdeenshire. This marriage also provided the Bruces with an important link with the Scottish royal family. In the 1290s, the Bruces as part of their claim to the Scottish throne during the 'Great Cause', 1291–2, claimed that King Alexander II of Scotland had recognised Robert Bruce (d. 1295), the grandfather of the future King, as his successor in 1238. No proof of this was forthcoming during the 'Great Cause', but it does seem that this Robert Bruce was acknowledged by the Scottish baronage as a likely successor in 1248–9 should the male line of the Scottish royal family die out.

Good marriages confirmed the Bruces' rise in status in the second half of the thirteenth century. In 1240, Robert, fifth Lord Annandale and grandfather of the future King, married as his first wife Isabel, daughter of Gilbert de Clare, Earl of Gloucester and Hertford, and sometime before 1280 married as his second wife Christina, daughter of William de Ireby

Loch Doon. Until damming in the 1950s the Bruce earldom of Carrick had a castle, Castle Doon, on an island in the loch. It was recaptured from the English in 1311.

of Cumberland. The latter marriage increased the Bruces' Cumberland connections as they already held land in this area by the second half of the twelfth century. Robert Bruce, the future King's father, was buried at Holm Cultram Abbey, Cumberland in 1304. More significant for the Bruce family's landed status in Scotland, however, was the marriage of this Robert, sixth Lord of Annandale and father of the future King, to the widowed Marjory, Countess of Carrick, between 1270 and 1272. This marriage, the fruits of which included the future King, took place in bizarre circumstances as described by John of Fordun (*Chronicle of the Scottish Nation*):

> one day, going out hunting at random, with her esquires and handmaidens, she met a gallant knight riding across the same country – a most seemly youth named Robert Bruce, son of Robert, surnamed the Bruce, the noble lord of Annandale in Scotland, and of Cleveland in England. When greetings and kisses had been given, on each side, as is the wont of courtiers, she besought him to stay and hunt and walk about; and seeing that he was rather unwilling to do so, she by force, so to speak, with her hand, made him pull up, and brought the knight, although very loath, to her castle of Turnberry with her. After dallying there, with the followers, for the space of fifteen days or more, he clandestinely took the countess to wife; while the friends and well-wishers of both knew nothing about it, nor had the king's consent been got at all in the matter. Therefore, the common belief of the whole country was that she had seized – by force as it were – this youth for her husband. . . . By means of the prayers of friends, however, and by a certain sum of money agreed upon, this Robert gained the king's goodwill, and the whole domain. Of Martha (Marjory) by God's providence, he begat a son who was to be the saviour, champion and king of the bruised Scottish people as the course of history will show.

Holm Cultram Abbey, Cumbria. In 1322 Robert Bruce plundered this Cistercian abbey 'notwithstanding that his father's body was buried there' (the *Lanercost Chronicle*).

The acquisition of the earldom of Carrick obviously strengthened the Bruce military presence in south-west Scotland. The head or caput of the earldom was at Turnberry Castle (Ayrshire), with Loch Doon Castle also having strategic significance. Robert Bruce, the future King, was born in 1274, probably at Turnberry Castle. His father resigned the earldom to him in 1292, well before his own death in 1304.

Robert Bruce, the future King, retained a strong association with the earldom of Carrick. He also inherited strong family associations with North Yorkshire, south Durham (i.e. Hartlepool) and Annandale. Above all, of course, he inherited a firm family belief in Bruce claims to the Scottish crown.

POLITICAL CRISIS AND THE POWER GAME

Tragedy struck Scotland in 1286 when King Alexander III died suddenly, aged forty-four years, on 18 March. He was accidentally killed on a stormy night on his way from Edinburgh to Kinghorn (Fife), where he intended to meet his new young French wife (of less than six months), Yolande of Dreux. The King lost his escorts on the rough coast road to Kinghorn during the storm and was eventually found dead, with a broken neck, on the shore.

At the time of this political crisis there were three Robert Bruces in Scotland – Robert, the fifth Lord of Annandale, known as the 'Competitor' because of his claim to the Scottish throne in 1291–2 (he died in 1295); his son, Robert, who became Earl of Carrick between 1270 and 1272 and although he resigned his earldom to his son, the future King, in 1292, he did not die until 1304; this Robert's son, the young Robert Bruce (future King), just twelve years of age in 1286. Only twenty years later he was to become King of Scots. According to Scottish tradition, Scotland descended into political chaos in 1286 after the 'Golden Age' of Alexander III before Robert Bruce rescued Scottish kingship in heroic fashion in 1306. However, this is a pro-Bruce interpretation of events before 1306, written after the event and to justify the Bruce coup of 1306. In 1286 the reality was very different and makes Bruce's eventual triumph after 1306 even more remarkable. In 1286 there was a settled political establishment of noble families who had worked with Alexander III since 1260 – these included the Comyns, Morays (or Murrays), Stewarts, Frasers, Macdougalls, Grahams, Balliols and Mowbrays. Despite the Bruces' increasing landed power and status in Scotland, they were *not* part of this political establishment in 1286 either at the centre, through political offices such as justiciar, chamberlain and chancellor, or in the localities through the office of sheriff. The Bruces had, in fact, played a more prominent role in English politics than Scottish politics during the second half of the thirteenth century. The family had held responsibilities such as the governorship of Carlisle Castle, 1267–8, and the sheriffdom of Cumberland, 1283–5, offices that complemented their landowning in that region. The Bruces, however, had increasing landed strength in south-west

Ruthven Castle. The substantial earthworks (now surmounted by eighteenth-century barracks) are testimony to the importance of the Comyns' thirteenth-century castle, the head of their Badenoch lordship.

Scotland and the status of Earls of Carrick in this region after 1272. More importantly, they had connections through marriage with the Scottish royal family and this needed to be asserted in 1286 when Alexander III's sudden death left the succession to the Scottish crown insecure.

In 1286, the heir to the throne was Alexander III's granddaughter, Margaret the Maid of Norway, a child of three years of age. Political leadership of the country was assumed by six guardians representing the political establishment of Alexander III's later years. The composition of this group was significant: it consisted of two earls (Alexander Comyn, Earl of Buchan, and Duncan, Earl of Fife), two bishops (William Fraser of St Andrews and Robert Wishart of Glasgow) and two barons (John Comyn of Badenoch and James Stewart). The dominance of the Comyn family is apparent, especially when it is noted that William Fraser, holder of the most important ecclesiastical office in Scotland, the bishopric of St Andrews, was an ally of the Comyns. It is notable that the Bruces were not members of this guardianship despite the fact that two members of the family, Robert Bruce of Annandale and Robert Bruce, Earl of Carrick, were major baronial figures. The Bruces' only link with political power in 1286 was their alliance, through marriage, with the Stewarts, who held a number of political offices.

Analysis of political office-holders in Alexander III's reign emphasises the political grip held by the Comyn family in particular by 1286. There were three branches of the Comyn family, the Comyn Earls of Buchan (since 1212), the Comyn Lords of Badenoch and Lochaber (since 1230) and the Comyn Lords of East Kilbride. Marriage alliances involving the two main branches – the Comyns of Badenoch and Buchan – had brought them, in the course of the thirteenth century, alliances with the earls of Mar, Ross, Dunbar, Angus, Strathearn and Fife and with the families of Balliol, Macdougall of Argyll, Moray, Mowbray and de Soules. Through family and other alliances, the Comyns dominated political offices at the centre and in the localities. Alexander Comyn, Earl of Buchan, was Justiciar of Scotia (the leading political office in the land) from 1258 until his death in 1289. The Comyns of Badenoch and Comyn allies, the Maxwells, were often associated with the justiciarship of Galloway; Comyn allies such as Hugh de Barclay and William de Soules held the justiciarship of Lothian. A succession of Comyn allies held the offices of chamberlain and chancellor. Comyns and their allies also controlled ecclesiastical offices in Alexander III's reign, especially the key office of the bishopric of St Andrews. Comyns and their allies dominated local government through control of many sheriffdoms. Alexander Comyn, Earl of Buchan, as well as being Justiciar of Scotia and Constable of Scotland was Sheriff of Wigtown (in the south-west) and Dingwall

Blair Castle. The medieval site at Blair Atholl, now covered by later buildings, was constructed by John Comyn, Lord of Badenoch, in 1269 to control the southern end of the Drumochter and Minigaig passes.

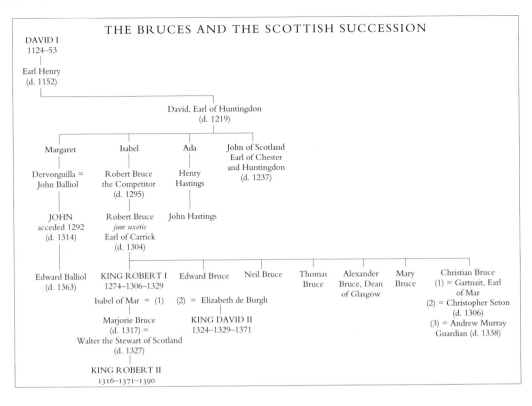

THE BRUCES AND THE SCOTTISH SUCCESSION

DAVID I
1124–53

Earl Henry
(d. 1152)

David, Earl of Huntingdon
(d. 1219)

Margaret

Dervorguilla =
John Balliol

JOHN
acceded 1292
(d. 1314)

Edward Balliol
(d. 1363)

Isabel

Robert Bruce
the Competitor
(d. 1295)

Robert Bruce
jure uxoris
Earl of Carrick
(d. 1304)

KING ROBERT I
1274–1306–1329

Ada

Henry
Hastings

John Hastings

Edward Bruce

John of Scotland
Earl of Chester
and Huntingdon
(d. 1237)

Neil Bruce

Thomas
Bruce

Alexander
Bruce, Dean
of Glasgow

Mary
Bruce

Christian Bruce
(1) = Gartnait, Earl
of Mar
(2) = Christopher Seton
(d. 1306)
(3) = Andrew Murray
Guardian (d. 1338)

Isabel of Mar = (1)   (2) = Elizabeth de Burgh

Marjorie Bruce
(d. 1317) =
Walter the Stewart of Scotland
(d. 1327)

KING DAVID II
1324–1329–1371

KING ROBERT II
1316–1371–1390

(in the north). Comyn influence was also felt in the sheriffdoms of Fife, Roxburgh, Dumfries, Forfar, Cromarty, Peebles, Edinburgh, Perth, Elgin, Kincardine, Lanark, Berwick, Dumbarton, Ayr and Banff.

The Comyns and their allies, through their own vast landholding and control of sheriffdoms, exercised immense control throughout Scotland by 1286. When this control is translated on to the Scottish landscape, it meant a network of private castles and royal castles that effectively dominated key lines of communication across many areas of Scotland. When used in alliance with the Scottish monarchy, this pattern of influence had helped to define Scottish royal authority in the west and north against Norwegian threats and also against revolt in the north from rival claimants to the Scottish throne. It would provide a stiff obstacle to the political ambitions of the Bruces.

What, in practice, stood in the way of the Bruces in the period 1286 to 1306? The military and political power of the Comyn family in northern Scotland was virtually vice-regal and was marked by a series of castles controlling most of the main routes and passes in northern Scotland. Their castles stretched from Inverlochy (Lochaber) in the west to Slains Castle, beside Collieston (Buchan), in the east. With the support of the Scottish monarchy, the Comyns were established as Earls of Buchan in 1212 and hereditary Lords of Badenoch (and Lochaber) in 1230 in order

THE COMYN FAMILY

The full scale of the Comyns vast network of influence is revealed by William Comyn Earl of Buchan's two marriages.

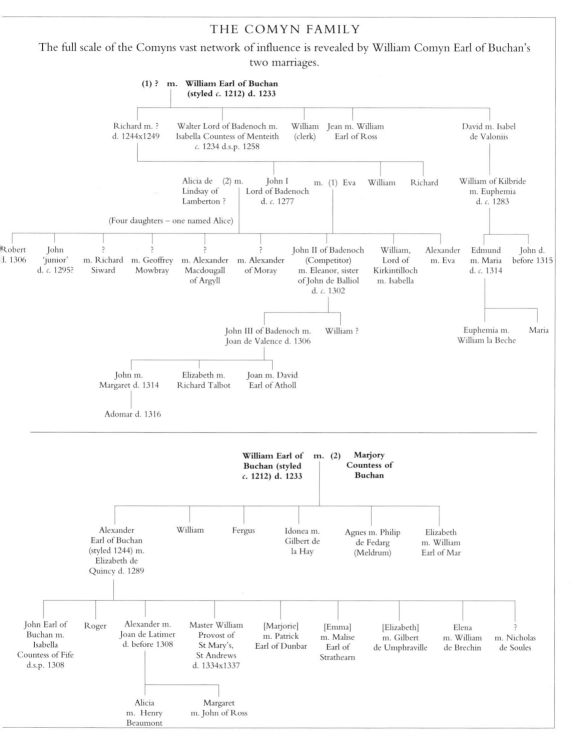

(1) ? m. William Earl of Buchan (styled c. 1212) d. 1233

- Richard m. ? d. 1244x1249
- Walter Lord of Badenoch m. Isabella Countess of Menteith c. 1234 d.s.p. 1258
- William (clerk)
- Jean m. William Earl of Ross
- David m. Isabel de Valoniis

Alicia de Lindsay of Lamberton ? (2) m. John I Lord of Badenoch d. c. 1277 m. (1) Eva — William — Richard — William of Kilbride m. Euphemia d. c. 1283

(Four daughters – one named Alice)

- Robert d. 1306
- John 'junior' d. c. 1295?
- ? m. Richard Siward
- ? m. Geoffrey Mowbray
- ? m. Alexander Macdougall of Argyll
- ? m. Alexander of Moray
- John II of Badenoch (Competitor) m. Eleanor, sister of John de Balliol d. c. 1302
- William, Lord of Kirkintilloch m. Isabella
- Alexander m. Eva
- Edmund m. Maria d. c. 1314
- John d. before 1315

John III of Badenoch m. Joan de Valence d. 1306 — William ?

Euphemia m. William la Beche — Maria

- John m. Margaret d. 1314
- Elizabeth m. Richard Talbot
- Joan m. David Earl of Atholl

Adomar d. 1316

William Earl of Buchan (styled c. 1212) d. 1233 m. (2) Marjory Countess of Buchan

- Alexander Earl of Buchan (styled 1244) m. Elizabeth de Quincy d. 1289
- William
- Fergus
- Idonea m. Gilbert de la Hay
- Agnes m. Philip de Fedarg (Meldrum)
- Elizabeth m. William Earl of Mar

- John Earl of Buchan m. Isabella Countess of Fife d.s.p. 1308
- Roger
- Alexander m. Joan de Latimer d. before 1308
- Master William Provost of St Mary's, St Andrews d. 1334x1337
- [Marjorie] m. Patrick Earl of Dunbar
- [Emma] m. Malise Earl of Strathearn
- [Elizabeth] m. Gilbert de Umphraville
- Elena m. William de Brechin
- ? m. Nicholas de Soules

- Alicia m. Henry Beaumont
- Margaret m. John of Ross

to strengthen royal authority in the north (especially in Moray) against revolt. It was, therefore, vital to the security of the area that Comyn castles controlled the strategically important passes from the north and west Highlands into the basin of the Tay. The key castles of the Comyn Lords of Badenoch and Lochaber – Ruthven, Lochindorb, Blair Atholl and Inverlochy – were all carefully sited and developed in the years after 1230.

Ruthven, the site now largely covered by the eighteenth-century Ruthven barracks, stands on a prominent hill, artificially scarped, rising from the flat floor of the Spey valley. Ruthven commanded the northern end of two passes over the Mounth, namely Drumochter and Minigaig. The southern end of these two passes was controlled by the castle at Blair Atholl built in 1269 by John Comyn I of Badenoch. The Drumochter pass was the most obvious route between Perth and Inverness. Lochindorb Castle was strategically situated in the heart of Moray on a loch between Forres and Grantown, occupying an island site covering 1 acre. With Inverlochy Castle, the chief castle of Lochaber, the Comyns presided over the entrance to the Great Glen, securing especially its southern sea outlet but also the overland route to the Spey by way of Glen Spean.

Comyn strategic control over northern Scotland was greatly enhanced by the castles of the Comyn Earls of Buchan. There are few visible

Drumochter Pass. A key communication link between Perth and Inverness, the pass was controlled by the Comyn castles of Ruthven (in the north) and Blair Atholl (in the south).

Lochindorb Castle. Meaning the 'Loch of Trouble' in Gaelic, Lochindorb is in the centre of Moray, on an island site. It was one of the chief thirteenth-century castles of the Comyns of Badenoch.

remains of these castles because of the famous 'herschip' or harrying of Buchan by Robert Bruce in 1308. However, the known Comyn castle sites in Buchan demonstrate by their position a formidable network of control. As a coastal earldom, it is not surprising to find Buchan defended by an impressive group of well-sited castles along its coastline. On the north coast, Dundarg was impressively positioned on a rock of red sandstone looking northwards over the outer reaches of the Moray Firth. East of Dundarg on the corner of Buchan, was Cairnbulg (its original name was Philorth) standing on a fairly prominent mound which was probably a motte. Further down the Buchan coast was Rattray, a strategically important motte site as it controlled what is thought to have been the port of Buchan. Further south (near Collieston) was Slains Castle.

Inland, a known Comyn castle in Buchan was Kingedward with its prominent site on a precipitous rock protected by the Kingedward burn on the south and on the north-west angle by a deep ditch which severed the neck of the peninsula. To strengthen further their castles in Buchan and Badenoch, the Comyn Earls of Buchan acquired and developed Balvenie Castle (Banffshire) between 1264 and 1282. Located only 20 miles from Badenoch's eastern border, it was an important bridge between Badenoch and Buchan. Perched on a promontory high above the River Fiddich, Balvenie Castle commanded the mouths of Glen Rinnes and Glenfiddich, the passes to Huntly, Keith and Cullen and the route to

Elgin. Of Comyn castles in northern Scotland, substantial remains exist only at Balvenie, Lochindorb and Inverlochy but there is evidence to indicate that a castle-building and development programme took place at all Comyn castle sites in the north between 1260 and 1286.

Though the Comyns are mainly associated with domination of northern Scotland, all three branches combined had considerable landed power (and castles) in central and southern Scotland. The Comyns of Badenoch held the Lordship of Kirkintilloch and Lenzie (Dumbarton-shire), which had a burgh and castle associated with it from the early thirteenth century. Kirkintilloch, on a former Roman site, was located strategically at the junctions of the Rivers Luggie and Kelvin. Further south, the Comyns of Badenoch held Dalswinton Castle, which commanded Nithsdale. In Roxburghshire, the family held Bedrule and Scraesburgh castles.

The Comyn Lords of East Kilbride had their main residence and castle at Kilbride, strengthening the family's influence in central Scotland, while the Comyns of Buchan greatly added to the family's presence in the south of Scotland when they inherited, in 1264, land from the great Anglo-Scottish landowner Roger de Quincy. This gave them important new territory especially in Galloway, but also in Cunningham, Lauderdale and Midlothian. The Comyns thus inherited, after 1264, the castle of Cruggleton in Galloway. Cruggleton was well situated on a cliff top. Though little remains of the Comyn castles of central and southern Scotland – only a single arch now survives at Cruggleton – control of the areas around Kirkintilloch, Dalswinton, Kilbride, Bedrule, Scraesburgh and Cruggleton was significant in the developing rivalry between Bruces and the Comyns in the south-west. Dalswinton lay close to the Bruce castle of Lochmaben and Cruggleton Castle was also near to the Bruce's earldom of Carrick – and to the strategically important Isle of Man, Scottish since 1266.

The considerable military, political and administrative strength represented by the Comyns' own castles was increased by their influence over key royal castles in their capacity as sheriffs. Comyn power in the north was strengthened further by their control over the sheriffdoms (and castles) of Banff (from the 1280s) and Dingwall. Their strength in the south-west (Galloway) was increased by their command of the sheriffdom of Wigtown. The Comyns' network of allies also added further control over royal castles and sheriffdoms with Dumfries, Elgin and Cromarty adding to the dominance of the Comyn-led government. Family alliances particularly enhanced the effectiveness of Comyn power in certain regions. Alliance with the Macdougall Lords of Argyll contributed key castles in the west, such as Dunstaffnage, Dunollie, Duart and Innis Chonnell in Loch Awe to Comyn dominance over this area. Similarly, the Balliol landowning power in the south-west, and the castle of Buittle, added to Comyn strength in the south-west.

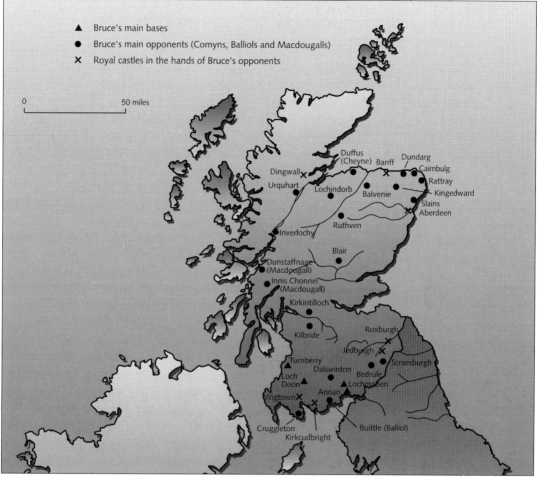

Main strongholds of Bruce's Scottish enemies.

Comyn power in the north was, in 1286, unassailable but the Bruces' own influence in the south-west meant that it was in this area that the Bruce challenge to the Comyns' control over Scottish government first took place. Comyn dominance had serious consequences for Bruce ambitions to gain power. The extreme youth of the heiress to the Scottish throne, the Maid of Norway, in 1286 seemed to ensure a long period of guardianship control over the Scottish government − and prolonged exclusion of Bruces from political office. In an age of high infant mortality, there needed to be some provision for an heir presumptive if the young Maid of Norway was to die. The Bruces' marriage links to the Scottish royal house in the thirteenth century gave them an interest in this. But how could they forward their claim when they were excluded from membership of the Guardianship, a grouping that was in the key position to implement the succession and influence the discussion over an heir

27

THE COMYNS: BRUCE'S GREATEST OPPOSITION

The period 1212 to 1314 could be described as the 'Comyn century' in Scottish history, such was the family's dominance of Scottish landholding and politics. By 1200 the family had territorial bases, through royal patronage, in southern Scotland (Roxburghshire and Peeblesshire) and central Scotland (Kirkintilloch). The family's rise to power was accelerated in the early thirteenth century when the Comyns became key royal agents for the consolidation of royal authority especially in northern Scotland. The elevation of the family to the earldom of Buchan in about 1212 became an important factor in exercising this role. From Buchan the Comyns were active against opponents of royal authority in Moray and Caithness.

Deer Abbey, Buchan. This austere Cistercian abbey was the religious centre of the Comyn earldom of Buchan. In 1267 the resigning abbot described it as a 'hovel'.

Dundarg Castle, Banffshire. One of the Comyn's coastal castles in thirteenth-century Buchan, Dundarg was destroyed by Bruce in 1308. Much of it was rebuilt in the sixteenth century.

The view from old Slains. Little survives of the thirteenth-century Comyn castle of Slains which stands on a promontory into the sea at Old Slains on the Buchan coast.

The Comyns naturally sought to mark their new status by visible symbols of their lordship. In 1219 William Comyn, Earl of Buchan, founded the Cistercian Abbey of Deer. Undoubtedly, this religious foundation was complemented by powerful symbols of secular lordship, i.e. castles. As a coastal earldom, Buchan was defended by an impressive group of well-sited castles along its coastline – Dundarg, Cairnbulg, Rattray, Slains – while inland Kingedward provided further strength. Robert Bruce's 'herschip' (harrying) of Buchan in 1308 left few visible remains to reflect the Comyn's earlier secular dominance.

Balvenie Castle, acquired by the Comyn earls of Buchan between 1264 and 1282, provided a strategic bridge between the Comyn bases of Buchan and Badenoch.

presumptive? The Comyns were allied through marriage to the Balliol family, who also had strong claims to the position of heir presumptive because of their own royal links. In the parliament of 2 April 1286, it appears that the aged Robert Bruce (d. 1295), the future King's grandfather, put forward his family's claim. 'A bitter pleading', i.e. an argument, ensued at another parliament later in April when the Balliols contested this claim. The Bruces' fear that the Guardians would not effectively represent their interests soon caused them to resort to strong-arm tactics: they launched attacks in south-west Scotland on the Balliol castle of Buittle and also the royal castles of Wigtown and Dumfries. These attacks on royal castles, controlled by the Comyns and their allies, show clear resistance to Comyn leadership of the political community of the realm.

Further evidence of the Bruces' defiance of the committee of Guardians, i.e. Scottish government, occurred in September 1286 when they made a pact with associates at Turnberry (the chief castle of Robert Bruce, Earl of Carrick). The pact involving Robert Bruce, Lord of Annandale (i.e. the future King's grandfather), his son Robert Bruce, Earl of Carrick (the future King's father), James Stewart (the Guardian), his brother John Stewart, Walter Stewart, Earl of Menteith and his sons, Patrick, Earl of Dunbar, Angus Macdonald, Lord of Islay and his son, was seemingly an agreement to support Richard de Burgh, Earl of Ulster and Thomas de Clare against their enemies. The pact involved keeping fealty to the English King and whoever should be King in Scotland, 'by reason of the blood of the Lord Alexander, King of Scotland according to the ancient customs hitherto approved and used in the kingdom of Scotland' (Turnberry Bond). Some historians have interpreted this as an indication of a deliberate bid by the Bruces for the Scottish throne. This is perhaps reading too much into the oath, which is not clear – in its vagueness, however, it certainly left open the possibility for a Bruce claim. Robert Bruce, the future King's grandfather, had after all been recognised, according to Bruce sources, as heir to Alexander II in 1238 by 'ancient custom'.

The Turnberry bond and the Bruce-inspired attacks on south-west castles were serious threats to the stability of Scottish government in 1286. The extent of the threat is made clear in the royal accounts of 1288–90. The account of John Comyn of Buchan as Sheriff of Wigtown refers specifically to the Earl of Carrick, Robert Bruce, the future King's father, as the instigator of war following Alexander III's death. Thus, the picture in Scottish tradition of Robert Bruce rescuing Scotland from twenty years of faction fighting is somewhat at odds with the reality – the Bruces were, in 1286, instigators of civil war against a well-established and experienced aristocratic government led by the Comyns.

Reaction to the Bruce threat to destabilise the Scottish government took a number of forms. The Comyns reinforced their own position in the south-west. Action was taken to strengthen royal castles not only in this area but also in the south, e.g. Ayr, Dumfries, Wigtown and Jedburgh, and at Edinburgh and Stirling. In 1288, John Comyn of Buchan, Earl Alexander's son, became keeper of the royal castle at Kirkcudbright in addition to that of Wigtown. John Comyn of Badenoch became Keeper of Jedburgh Castle, complementing his own private castles at Bedrule and Scraesburgh. The Guardians put the national army on twenty-four-hour alert and sent out embassies to Edward I in France asking for his advice and assistance. Edward I began to involve himself in Scottish affairs on his return from France in 1289 when negotiations began between Scottish, Norwegian and English representatives for the future marriage between the young Maid of Norway and Edward I's son. At this point, Robert Bruce of Annandale joined three Guardians as the Scottish envoys and it seems that some sort of conciliation between Bruce and the representatives of Scottish government had been brokered by Edward I. The situation for all involved in Scottish politics changed considerably, however, when the young 'Queen' Margaret died in Orkney in September 1290 on her way from Norway to Scotland. There was no agreed successor.

The experienced William Fraser, Bishop of St Andrews, a close ally of the Comyns in the Scottish government, wrote to Edward I informing him of the new political instability in Scotland and that Robert Bruce the elder (the future King's grandfather) with his supporters, the earls of Mar and Atholl, had gathered a large armed force and had come to Perth. He asked Edward to intervene 'to save the shedding of blood' and recommended John Balliol to him as the best candidate for the throne. Clearly, the political establishment in Scotland would favour the claims of John Balliol, the brother-in-law of John Comyn of Badenoch. The Bruces were also aware of the value of the English King's support. In the winter of 1290–1 the elder Bruce asked Edward I to support him as the choice of 'the Seven Earls'. The years 1286–8 had shown that the Bruces had an insufficient power base to achieve power in Scotland by force. Thus, in 1290, the elder Bruce ingeniously introduced the ancient constitutional concept of 'the Seven Earls' to suggest that his claim to the Scottish throne was backed within Scotland by the whole body of the earls and that this body had a right in elections. The 'Appeal', which is weakened by the fact that only two earls (Fife and Mar) are named, asserted a wider political support for Bruce and argued that John Comyn and William Fraser, Bishop of St Andrews, did not represent 'the whole community of the realm' but were acting by 'private authority'. Bruce tried to claim the high moral ground. The two urgent appeals to Edward I from two rival political forces in Scotland, reminiscent of the situation in Scotland during the minority of Alexander III in the 1250s, gave Edward I every reason to believe that his intervention was welcome and that he could use the opportunity to insist on his recognition as lord superior of Scotland.

Inverlochy Castle lay beneath Ben Nevis, viewed here across Loch Linnhe.The Comyns of Badenoch held the adjoining lordship of Lochaber from this key strategic base near to Fort William.

Norham Castle, the chief border stronghold of the bishop of Durham. This castle withstood three prolonged sieges between 1318 and 1322 and its garrison inflicted damage on Scottish forces.

Spean Valley. The Comyns controlled the important Spean Valley route to the Spey from their castle at Inverlochy.

The Great Glen and Loch Lochy. This was one of the most important communication networks in northern Scotland and vital to secure for control of the north.

33

Buittle Castle, near Dalbeatie, was the chief centre of the Balliol lordship in eastern Galloway. Dervorguilla de Balliol formulated the Statutes of Balliol College, Oxford, there in 1282.

Edward came to Norham in June 1291 so that 'by virtue of the overlordship which belongs to him he may do justice to everyone'. The Guardians refused to acknowledge Edward I's overlordship – they had recently negotiated the Treaty of Birgham with Edward I (signed in July 1290) in which the right of Scotland to its independence, its own rights, laws, liberties and customs was recognised. Subsequently, the Guardians maintained their insistence on Scottish independence 'in the name of the community of the realm of Scotland'. However, Edward cleverly outflanked the leaders of the political community by getting the thirteen claimants to the Scottish throne to agree that he was their rightful overlord and that they would abide by his judgement on the succession.

A court was appointed to decide which of the thirteen claimants or 'Competitors' had the best right to the Scottish throne and this met for the first time in August 1291 – the lawsuit, which came to be known as the 'Great Cause' in the eighteenth century, had begun. Of the thirteen candidates, it was clear at the time that the two most serious candidates were John Balliol and Robert Bruce, the elder. The drama of the legal confrontation between Balliol and Bruce and the consequent events has generated both legends and misconceptions. Subsequent Bruce propaganda, for instance, has given rise to a long-lasting tradition that Balliol was a puppet nominated by Edward I to the Scottish kingship in

Sweetheart Abbey, Nithsdale. Founded in 1273 by the rich and pious Dervorguilla de Balliol in honour of her husband John (d. 1268), the abbey suffered damage in the Anglo-Scottish war.

Glen Rinnes. This glen was effectively controlled by the Comyn castle of Balvenie (see pages 29 and 111), which lay at its mouth.

Buittle church. The wealth of the Balliol family is demonstrated in their architectural patronage of this church, much of which dates to their lordship between 1234 and 1296.

Innis Chonnel Castle. Strategically situated on an island in Loch Awe, this thirteenth-century castle was held by John Macdougall against Bruce in the early fourteenth century.

defiance of a national belief that Bruce had a better claim. If Balliol was a puppet, however, he was a puppet of the dominant Comyn group in Scottish government who would strengthen their power if the Balliol candidature was successful. In the legal battle, Bruce was allowed to nominate forty auditors and Balliol and Comyn together a further forty. An analysis of this latter group reveals a predominantly Comyn following rather than a Balliol following – the names of Comyn relatives and allies dominate the list. What is more, the nominees of Balliol and Comyn represent, by their office-holding, the key officers of the Scottish government. John Balliol appeared to be the official government candidate supported also by most of the ecclesiastical hierarchy.

In practice, therefore, the Bruce legal challenge in the 'Great Cause' (1291–2) was another stage in the battle for political power in Scotland. The final decision of the court, on 17 November 1292, went in favour of John Balliol. Legally he had a better case by the principles of primogeniture – the Balliol cause claimed seniority of line against the Bruces' claim of nearness of degree. The weakness of the Bruces' legal case can be seen by the 'many and varied' arguments they adopted when compared to the short, focused case of Balliol. As for Edward I, in his role as overlord, he seems to have favoured the political party that had the most widespread support and seemed most capable of bringing stability to Scotland. This candidate was John Balliol, the choice of the Comyn-led government. The Comyns would, undoubtedly, be the real power behind the kingship of John Balliol. Despite the use of military and legal means to strengthen their political position between 1286 and 1292, the Bruces had failed to dislodge the Comyns from their position of dominance. Yet they ensured that they would retain their claim to the throne. Before the final verdict, but as soon as the court decided against the elder Bruce, the Competitor, and for Balliol on the issue of seniority versus nearness of degree on 5 and 6 November 1292, the elder Bruce resigned his claim (on 7 November) to his son and heir and in turn to his heirs. On 9 November 1292, Robert Bruce, Earl of Carrick, in turn, surrendered his earldom to his son and heir, Robert (the future King) then aged just eighteen years.

BRUCE, WALLACE AND THE SCOTTISH WARS

John Balliol was enthroned King of Scots on St Andrew's Day (30 November 1292). The threat of Bruce opposition had been apparent on 7 November when Bruce the Competitor preserved his family's claim by resigning it, before the final decision in favour of Balliol, to his son and his successors. This threat became reality when the two elder Bruces, the future King's father and grandfather, refused to do homage to John Balliol as Scottish King. It is interesting, however, to note that the young Robert Bruce, the future king, did homage to Balliol, a necessity if he was to be confirmed as Earl of Carrick. This took place at the Stirling parliament of August 1293 with the support of Bruce allies, James Stewart and the Earl of Mar.

Discussion of John Balliol's kingship has been dominated by the legend of Balliol as an ineffective puppet of Edward I, a picture created, in fact, by pro-Bruce Scottish writers of the fourteenth and fifteenth centuries. According to this tradition, also, Robert Bruce the Competitor had not only a better right to the kingship of Scotland than Balliol, he had, in fact, been promised the kingship by Edward I. Further, as later stated by John of Fordun in the *Chronicle of the Scottish Nation*, on the eve of the Scottish Wars in 1296, Edward I had called Robert Bruce the grandfather to him – in reality this must have been Robert Bruce's father rather than the grandfather (who died in 1295) – and 'acknowledged that he had given an unrighteous sentence'. There is no evidence, however, to confirm this version of events, which appears likely to have been pro-Bruce propaganda of the fourteenth century.

The reality that faced young Robert Bruce, the future King, in 1292 was that the Bruces had been thwarted by the rules of primogeniture rather than cheated out of their rights. The Comyn-led aristocracy of Scotland had had their candidate, Balliol, confirmed as King and their own power in Scottish government consolidated at the same time. The inner core of advisers surrounding John Balliol and in public offices comprised the same figures who were influential in the later years of Alexander III's reign (1249–86) and through the Guardianship (1286–91) – John Comyn of Badenoch, brother-in-law to the new

Duffus Castle, Moray. A very fine example of a twelfth-century motte (mound) and bailey (courtyard) castle, Duffus was held by Reginald Cheyne, Warden of Moray and a Comyn ally in 1307.

Scottish King, and his cousin John Comyn, Earl of Buchan (following his father Alexander's death in 1289) were of central importance, the latter holding the main administrative office of Justiciar of Scotia as well as the office of Constable. Others who wielded considerable influence were Comyn family relatives such as Geoffrey Mowbray (Justiciar of Lothian), Alexander de Balliol (Chancellor), Alexander Macdougall (who held wide-ranging powers over Kintyre, Argyll and Lewis) and Comyn associates such as William Earl of Ross, the Frasers, Umphravilles and Grahams. Outside the large group of Comyn associates, the Stewarts continued to thrive in government. The first parliament of Balliol's reign in February 1293 sought to consolidate royal authority in the north and west by giving further power to three of these families through the creation of three new sheriffdoms. Alexander Macdougall was to be Sheriff of Lorn, a sheriffdom to be governed from his castle at Dunstaffnage. The sheriffdom of Skye was to be placed under the authority of William Earl of Ross and the sheriffdom of Kintyre was to be under the control of James Stewart.

Yet the authority of this experienced government under Balliol's kingship was to be tested not only by internal opposition – the Macdonalds in the Hebrides as well as the two elder Bruces had refused to acknowledge Balliol's kingship and render homage – but also by the increasingly interventionist role of Edward I as overlord of Scotland. Edward I had fulfilled his promise to the new ruler in Scotland to hand over the kingdom within two months of the final judgement. His role in Scotland, however, was complicated immediately by the fact that he had ruled Scotland directly between June 1291 and November 1292 and, naturally, there were financial and judicial matters from that time to be settled. Edward I felt that he still had the right to intervene directly on these and other matters. It is also clear that he sought to control Scotland by exerting influence over the leading landowning and political power in Scotland, the Comyns. During his direct rule in Scotland, Edward I must have been aware of the capacity of the Comyns and their allies to control key lines of communication in Scotland through their castle holding. In addition to their private castle holding, for instance, the Comyns alone held a number of royal castles in 1291: John Comyn, Earl of Buchan, held Wigtown (in Galloway); Kirkcudbright, Banff and Aberdeen, while his brother Alexander held Dingwall; John Comyn of Badenoch held Jedburgh, Clunie, Dull, Kilbride and Brideburgh (Barburgh in Dumfriesshire). In about 1293 Edward I sought to harness this power by a marriage alliance linking John Comyn, the younger of Badenoch, with Joan de Valence, daughter of William, Earl of Pembroke, and cousin of

Carlisle Castle. In the keeping of Robert Bruce's father (on the English side when war broke out in 1296), the castle's defences defied Wallace in 1297 and Bruce in 1315.

the English King. He was also not slow to remind both John Balliol and John Comyn, Earl of Buchan, of their financial obligations owing to him as their overlord in respect of their inherited lands in Scotland.

Edward I had, however, underestimated the determination of the Comyn-led political community to defend the rights, laws, liberties and customs of the Scottish kingdom. Soon after Balliol's enthronement, Edward asserted his right to hear whatever appeals from Scotland might be brought to him; he could even summon the Scottish King himself. When the Scottish political community reminded him of the promises made in the Treaty of Birgham (1289), 'the realm of Scotland shall remain separated and divided and free in itself . . . the rights, laws and liberties and customs of the realm to be preserved in every respect', Edward's unambiguous reply asserted his new rights as overlord since June 1291. He had the right to review decisions made by the Scottish Guardians and any promises made by him in the interregnum, i.e. the Treaty of Birgham, were no longer binding. In these circumstances it is hardly surprising that those in Scotland with grievances against the political establishment there would make them known to Edward. Thus, the Macdonalds (who had grievances against the Macdougalls), Simon Restalrig (who had a dispute with Patrick Graham) and relatives of the Earl of Fife (who had grievances against the Abernethys) were among those who appealed to the English King.

The Bruces, too, were to turn to the English King to fulfil their ambitions in Scotland. They demonstrated their own strength in south-west Scotland by having their candidate, Master Thomas Dalton of Kirkcudbright, elected as Bishop of Galloway in 1294 despite the objections of John Balliol, as King and Lord of Galloway. They also sought alliances outside Scotland. In 1293 Robert Bruce's father went to Norway, with Edward I's agreement, to give his daughter, Isabella, in marriage to King Eric of Norway. However, the outbreak of war between England and France in June 1294 set off a chain of events that would demonstrate very forcibly the Bruces' allegiance to the English King. Edward, using his full power as 'Lord Superior of the kingdom of Scotland', summoned John Balliol, ten Scottish earls and sixteen barons to perform personal feudal service against the French. Not since 1159, when the young Malcolm IV had joined Henry II's army at Toulouse, had a King of Scotland displayed such subordination by performing overseas military service for a King of England. The Scottish political community sought external help, an alliance with France, in order to preserve the rights, customs and independence of the Scottish kingdom. The treaty signed in October 1295 and ratified by a Scottish parliament in February 1296 was, in effect, a declaration of war on England. Further, the Scottish political community took power out of the hands of John Balliol and replaced him by a Council of Twelve. Balliol, despite tutoring by those who wielded political power in Scotland, had proven to be weak, inexperienced and vacillating when faced personally with Edward I on the issue of appeals to England in October 1293. He seemed to be similarly fragile on the question of Scottish service against France. He could not be trusted to represent the Scottish political community in practice, though he still remained the symbol of independent Scottish kingship and nationhood.

Where did the Bruces, the future King and his father, stand in 1295? Even before the Scottish government, in the name of John Balliol, had summoned the host to assemble on 22 March 1296 outside Selkirk, the Bruces had committed themselves to Edward I. Already by October 1295, Edward I was preparing for military action against opposition to him in Scotland. As part of this, he committed to Robert Bruce, Lord of Annandale (the future King's father), the keeping of the castle of Carlisle on 6 October 1295. Thus, Robert Bruce and his son, as well as Patrick, Earl of Dunbar, and Gilbert de Umphraville, Earl of Angus, did homage to Edward I and refused the Scottish summons: 'we are and always have been faithful to, and subject to, the will of the most noble prince and our beloved lord, Edward . . . we will serve him well and loyally against all men'. As a result, the Scottish government, according to the *Lanercost Chronicle*, 'pronounced forfeiture of his paternal heritage upon Robert de

Overleaf:
Sweetheart Abbey, Nithsdale. The abbey was probably not completed before the Scottish war started. Like other castles and abbeys in south-west Scotland, Sweetheart Abbey (especially its lands) suffered extensive damage at the hands of English soldiers.

Dunbar Castle. Although a very important castle from the beginning of the Anglo-Scottish war, there are few medieval remains. It was ruined by Order of Parliament in 1567.

Brus the younger, who had fled to England, because he would not do homage to them. Also, they forfeited his son in the earldom of Carrick, wherein he had been infeft, because he adhered to his father.' The Bruce lordship in south-west Scotland passed to their enemies the Comyns through John Comyn, Earl of Buchan.

At the outset of the Scottish Wars, or the Wars of Independence as they are most commonly known, it was the Comyns and their allies who represented Scottish nationhood and independence. The Bruces, including the future King, were on the English side. Given the rivalry between the Comyns and the Bruces, it was hardly surprising that one of the first actions of the war, on 26 March 1296, was an attack by a Scottish force from Annandale led by John Comyn, Earl of Buchan, six other Scottish earls and John Comyn, the younger, of Badenoch on Carlisle where Robert Bruce senior was in charge of the garrison. The Carlisle raid was repulsed and John Comyn, Earl of Buchan, returned to Sweetheart Abbey. At about the same time, an English army was gathering around Berwick and on 30 March the town, then only surrounded by a ditch and timber palisade for defence, was attacked and many townsmen (according to one, very exaggerated, account over 11,000) were butchered. In revenge, the Scots based at Jedburgh and under the leadership of the Earls of Mar, Ross and Menteith raided Northumberland, particularly Redesdale, Coquetdale and Tynedale, committing many atrocities. English propaganda states that the Scots burned alive some 200 schoolboys at Corbridge, though it is more probable the town was Hexham and that they were guilty of no more than arson.

Following this raid, the Scots on their way back took Dunbar with the help of the Countess of Dunbar, a member of the Comyn family who, unlike her husband, had remained loyal to the Scottish government. The town was subsequently besieged by the English force. It was at Dunbar on 27 April that the first phase of the Scottish wars took a decisive turn when the main Scots army trying to relieve the siege of the castle was routed and the Scots within the castle also surrendered. Scottish casualties at Dunbar were estimated at 10,000 dead, an undoubted exaggeration, but the severity of the Scottish defeat was certain and a large number of important figures in Scottish government were taken prisoner. Scottish resistance after Dunbar was negligible – key Scottish castles such as Roxburgh, Edinburgh and Stirling soon surrendered. The *Lanercost Chronicle* reported that at Stirling Edward I found 'the castle evacuated for fear of him, the keys hanging above the open doors'. According to a contemporary account (reproduced in J. Steventon (ed.), *Documents Illustrative of the History of Scotland, 1286–1306*) Edward 'conquered the realm of Scotland and searched it . . . within twenty one weeks without any more'. Edward marched north through Scotland via Perth, Montrose, Banff and Elgin, receiving fealty from most Scottish nobles and knights. On 8 July at Montrose, John Balliol formally submitted to Edward I, resigning his

Newcastle Castle. The arrival of the railway in 1849 considerably affected the castle site and the main medieval remains now comprise the keep (late twelfth century) and the gatehouse (Black Gate, mid-thirteenth century).

Berwick Castle. The castle resisted Bruce's attempts to capture it in 1312 and 1316 before capitulating in 1318, allowing the Scots easier access to northern England.

Urquhart Castle. Most extant buildings date from 1509 but the castle was built in the mid-thirteenth century by the Durwards. The Comyns had control of it before Bruce captured it in 1307.

kingdom to the English King and having his coat of royal arms stripped from his tabard in public – humiliating circumstances which resulted in his nickname in Scottish tradition 'Toom Tabard' ('Empty Surcoat').

The absence of the Bruces from the Scottish side at the first major engagement of the Scottish Wars caused some difficulty for the fourteenth- and fifteenth-century chroniclers, John of Fordun and Walter Bower, to whom Robert Bruce, the future King, was the ultimate hero and defender of Scottish nationhood against English imperialism. According to Fordun (the *Chronicle of the Scottish Nation*), Bruces' actions in 1296, as well as the Scottish capitulation, can be explained thus: '[Edward I] promised and pledged himself to the said Robert the grandfather [though the future king's father is probably meant as the grandfather died in 1295] to promote him to the throne as having the better and stronger right, while the other [John Balliol] should be set aside and deprived for ever. By this promise . . . he led him to write a letter himself to all his friends dwelling in Scotland and advise them to surrender and deliver up to him all castles and fortified strongholds.' This undoubtedly exaggerates the Bruces' national influence in 1296. The Bruces after 1292, apart from the young Robert Bruce, the future King, were political exiles from Scotland. Their hopes of fulfilling their long-held claims to the Scottish kingship rested, in practice, with the English King to whom they all gave very active service in 1295 and 1296. Fordun reported after the English victory at Dunbar that 'the elder Bruce (the future King's father) came up to the King of England and besought him to fulfil faithfully what he had long ago promised him, as to his getting the kingdom'. Edward's famous reply – '. . . in no little indignation . . . "Have we nothing else to do but win kingdoms for thee?" ' – made it clear that Edward was not simply prepared to replace Balliol with Bruce. King Edward now intended to rule Scotland directly.

The most well-defined demonstration of Edward I's policy of direct rule was the removal of the Stone of Destiny, the most precious symbol of Scottish monarchy and Scottish nationhood from Scone Abbey to Westminster Abbey. This rankled long in Scottish memory as Scottish kings had been inaugurated on the Stone for centuries. Over 650 years later, in the early hours of Christmas 1950, a group of young

Stirling Castle, the key stronghold linking northern and southern Scotland. It was to relieve Stirling Castle from Edward Bruce's siege that Edward II marched north in 1314.

Scots took the Stone from Westminster and brought it back to Scotland. The Stone was hidden away until April 1951, and was buried at Arbroath Abbey for the police to find and return to Westminster, although it was again returned to Scotland (Edinburgh Castle) in 1998. Apart from the Stone, other Scottish muniments and government records were also taken to London. However, more significant for the future leadership of the patriot nationalist movement in Scotland was the absence of key members of the Scottish government, who were captured and taken to England. Eight members of the dominant Comyn family were imprisoned south of the border as well as their King, John Balliol. Members of the Mowbray, Moray, Macdougall, Graham, Balliol, Randolph, Sinclair, Cheyne, Lochore, Ros, Mowat and Airth families who had supported the Balliol-Comyn government at the centre or in the localities were also confined in England.

Edward I refused to fill the political vacuum with the Bruces. Instead he appointed English officials to key roles: John de Warenne as his Lieutenant (keeper) of Scotland, Hugh Cressingham as Treasurer and Walter Amersham as Chancellor. He appears to have concentrated his resources mainly south of the Forth, establishing his centre for the administration of Scotland at Berwick and ensuring all major castles in the south, including Comyn and Balliol castles, were under English control. In the north he seems to have used a mixture of English officials and Scots who, he hoped, would be cowed into support by the imprisonment of family members in England. Walter Bower (*Scotichronicon*), writing in the fifteenth century, was probably correct in judging that the English King thought himself 'safe as a result of the abject submission of the Scots' in 1296. By May 1297 this judgement was proven to be wrong. Opposition to the English presence manifested itself in a series of revolts in the north and south-west. The period 1296–7 also saw the emergence of both William Wallace and Robert Bruce, the younger and future King, who both attempted to fill the vacuum in the leadership of the Scottish political community brought about by the imprisonment of the Comyns and so many of their associates after the fall of Dunbar.

The revolts have usually been seen as either aristocratic, inspired by supporters of the Bruce cause, i.e. Robert Bruce, the younger, James Stewart and Robert Wishart, Bishop of Glasgow, or as spontaneous 'popular' revolts led by William Wallace and Andrew Moray. The role of the young Robert Bruce on the 'nationalist' side is significant but has been overestimated. The involvement of individuals and families who had had a prominent role in Scottish government before English direct rule is of greater importance – James Stewart and Bishop Wishart had acted as Scottish Guardians; the Macdougall and Moray families had played key roles in the government of John Balliol. Revolt in Scotland started in the north early in 1297. Both Stewart and Macdougall power in the west and

The South Tyne valley. This area was troubled by Scottish raids from both William Wallace (1297) and Robert Bruce (1311). Bruce resumed Scottish royal control over the lordship of Tynedale in 1314.

Clifford's Tower, York.
In 1298, York Castle was
prepared to receive Edward I's
government – the Exchequer
was to be housed in the hall,
the Receipt in the tower and
the judicial bench situated in a
temporary structure.

north-west as government agents was seriously threatened by Edward I's attempt to extend English influence in the area by appointing Alexander Macdonald of Islay in April 1296 as Baillie of Kintyre (formerly under James Stewart's jurisdiction) and Baillie in the sheriffdoms of Lorn, Ross and the Isles (formerly under the control of Alexander Macdougall of Argyll). Edward I must have assumed that there would not be a threat from the Macdougalls as Alexander Macdougall was a prisoner in Berwick Castle. The Macdougall revolt was led by Alexander's son, Duncan, who had never sworn fealty to Edward I. Duncan received support from the strategic Comyn castle of Inverlochy (with its two galleys outside) in his resistance to Macdonald's attempts to control this area.

The Stewarts had even greater cause for grievance against the English king. The family had greatly increased its political responsibilities in the west during Alexander III's reign and later in John Balliol's reign. The early submission of James Stewart to Edward I in 1296, shortly after the battle at Dunbar, was, no doubt, designed to retain some favour with Edward I. The English King, on his part, seemed to be attempting to consolidate Stewart loyalty by arranging a marriage alliance between James Stewart and the sister of one of Edward's closest supporters, the de Burgh family, Earls of Ulster. In practice, Stewart lost political control (and power) in the south-west as well as the west to Edward I's agents. In addition to their losses to the Macdonalds, Stewart's political status in the west suffered as a result of Edward's appointment of Henry Percy as English Warden of Ayr and Galloway after September 1296.

Significant resistance to Edward's administration came from another family that had been involved in Scottish government before 1296, the Morays. Andrew de Moray of Petty had been Justiciar of Scotia during the Balliol kingship and his authority in 1296 can be judged by his imprisonment in the Tower of London. His son, Andrew, had also been detained, at Chester, but after his escape led a very successful campaign against English castles in northern Scotland. Between May and July 1297, the major castles of Inverness, Urquhart, Banff, Elgin and Aberdeen had fallen to young Andrew de Moray.

Compared to the Stewart, Macdougall and Moray families who had all lost power because of Edward I and were justifiably resentful of his English administration in Scotland, it is rather more difficult to explain the involvement of Robert Bruce, the future King. Bruce had, after all, been exiled by the Scottish government along with his father, who had refused to swear fealty to Balliol; they had both been on Edward I's side at the outbreak of the Scottish Wars. The fact that Edward I showed no inclination to reward the Bruces with any political responsibilities in Scotland (let alone the kingship itself) may have persuaded the younger Bruce to join the revolt in the south-west after it started. The *Guisborough Chronicle* reports that the Bishop of Carlisle had doubts about Bruce's loyalty after the Scottish revolt started and asked him to take a special oath of allegiance. The chronicler then explained that Robert Bruce joined the Scots because he was a Scotsman. It is interesting that Bruce tried to rally the support of his father's vassals in Annandale but they were unwilling to support him because their lord, Bruce's father, remained loyal to Edward I. The *Guisborough Chronicle* suggests that Bruce was already aiming at the Scottish throne in 1297, but it seems more probable that Bruce was initially trying to establish himself as one of the leaders of the Scottish political community. His status as Earl of Carrick gave him military resources that would be valuable to the revolt. Bruce also actively sought to associate himself with his more politically experienced allies, Stewart and Wishart. This strategy was sensible in view of the absence of the Comyns and their allies in England.

Robert Bruce's first appearance in the 'national' cause ended rather ignominiously with the capitulation of Bruce, Stewart and Wishart at Irvine in early July 1297. Surrender negotiations lasted for some time and one of the conditions of Bruce's submission was, apparently, that he ceded his only child, Marjorie (only a few years old at that time). It seems that Bruce still had not formally yielded by November 1297 and he probably neither submitted nor surrendered his daughter.

Cockermouth Castle, Cumbria. The castle is strategically situated between the rivers Derwent and Cocker but had become dilapidated and in need of extensive repair by 1316.

Bamburgh Castle. This stronghold acted as a valuable refuge from Scottish raids – Bamburgh people were said to fold up their wooden houses and carry them into the castle.

Compared to the ineptitude of the aristocratic revolt in the south-west, the so-called 'popular' revolts of William Wallace and Andrew de Moray were outstandingly successful. Too much contrast has been made between the 'official' revolt of Wishart, Stewart and Bruce on the one hand and the revolts of Moray and Wallace on the other. The young Andrew de Moray was a member of a well-established aristocratic family and William Wallace was himself from a knightly family in the feudal following of James Stewart. Thus James Stewart seems to be the focus for the involvement (for different reasons) of both Robert Bruce and William Wallace in the 1297 revolt. Both the *Lanercost Chronicle* and *Guisborough Chronicle* agree that James Stewart and Bishop Wishart caused 'a certain bloody man, William Wallace, who had formerly been a chief of brigands in Scotland to revolt against the king and assemble the people in revolt.' Both the revolt of William Wallace in the south and that of Andrew de Moray in the north had popular support. This is hardly surprising given Edward I's demands on the population as a whole for greater financial exactions, the seizure of wool stores as well as compulsory military service from 'all the middle people in Scotland' in Edward's French wars. Popular support for Wallace and Moray was increased by their military success.

Edward I's reaction to the revolts in Scotland in the first half of 1297 is rather surprising. His policy towards Scotland in this year seems to have been affected by the greater priority he placed upon his campaign against the French in Flanders. He promised release to Scottish prisoners in England if they pledged to serve him in Flanders. In addition, in late June 1297, he asked three members of the Comyn family, John Comyn, Earl of Buchan, with his brother Alexander and John Comyn, Lord of Badenoch, to help quell the revolt in Scotland. John, Earl of Buchan, and Alexander of Buchan were to counter the rebellion of their associate Andrew de Moray in the north while John Comyn of Badenoch was commanded to assist Brian fitz Alan in the custody of the kingdom and especially the defence of Roxburgh. Edward must have felt that the Comyns had been duly chastened by their period of imprisonment in England and would use their vast influence to restore order to Scotland. Letters from Edward I's officers in July and August 1297 cast doubt that the Comyns were actively pursuing Edward's orders. According to the *Guisborough Chronicle*, John Comyn, Earl of Buchan, 'at first pretended to repress rebellion but in the end changed sides and became a thorn in our flesh'. The Comyns did not come out openly in support of the Scottish rebellion until late 1297 – two members of the family were, after all, serving in Edward I's army in Flanders (they deserted early in 1298). The Comyn network of influence was so vast, however, that it is unlikely that Moray could have gathered a large infantry force in the north and joined Wallace's force in the south by September 1297 without Comyn co-operation.

The combined forces of Wallace and Moray won a famous victory over English forces led by the Treasurer, Hugh de Cressingham, and John de Warenne, Earl of Surrey, at Stirling Bridge on 11 September 1297. The battle took place on ground that is now built over but the general site can be viewed from Stirling Castle. The bridge that gives its name to the battle was a wooden one close to the present 'old bridge', which was built in the sixteenth century and is still used by pedestrians. Wallace and Moray took up their position about a mile north-east of the original wooden bridge, which was only wide enough for two horses to cross. English leadership at the battle was grossly negligent – the Earl of Surrey apparently sent away part of his army because the Treasurer had complained of the expense; the Earl himself caused a delay by oversleeping and then chose to save time by using the narrow bridge to cross the river instead of the ford 2 miles away where sixty men could cross at once. According to the *Lanercost Chronicle* 'the Scots allowed as many Englishmen to cross the bridge as they could hope to overcome, and then, having blocked the bridge, they slaughtered all who crossed over, among whom perished the Treasurer of England, Hugh de Cressingham, of whose skin William Wallace caused a broad strip to be taken from the head to the heel, to make therewith a baldrick for his sword'.

The victory at Stirling Bridge gave Andrew de Moray and William Wallace, in practice, the leadership of the Scottish political community. They re-established the Scottish Guardianship as a distinctly military regime with two proven martial commanders replacing the traditional political leadership of the Comyns and Stewarts which had been found wanting, militarily, in 1296 and 1297. The leadership of Moray and Wallace was highly conscious of the need to raise money for the war effort. A letter from Moray and Wallace as 'leaders of the army of the kingdom of Scotland' and from the 'community of that kingdom' assured the mayor and communities of Lübeck and Hamburg that, after Stirling Bridge, they again had safe access to Scottish ports. Andrew de Moray died in November 1297 of wounds received at Stirling Bridge. Owing to his early death, Moray's role in 1297 has tended to be overshadowed by Wallace, who was subsequently knighted and appointed sole Guardian of the kingdom. In his acts of government, Wallace was clearly acting on behalf of John Balliol, whom he regarded as the rightful king: 'William Wallace, knight, Guardian of the kingdom of Scotland and commander of its army, in the name of the famous prince the lord John, by God's grace illustrious king of Scotland, by consent of the community of that kingdom'.

Wallace led the political community of Scotland until his defeat at the Battle of Falkirk (22 July 1298). As the letter to the merchants of Lübeck and Hamburg had revealed, the Scots needed funds for the war effort. Another method of raising money quickly was to raid and loot the lands bordering on Scotland. According to the northern English *Lanercost*

YORK AND THE SCOTTISH WARS

York city walls, Nunnery Lane. Urgent attention was given to strengthening York's stone walls in the late thirteenth and early fourteenth centuries in the face of the Scottish threat.

Yrk's role as a war capital following William Wallace's victory at the Battle of Stirling Bridge in 1297 had a considerable physical impact on the city. Bruce's victory at Bannockburn (1314) meant that the whole of northern England, including Yorkshire, was threatened by Scottish raids and York became a frontier town in need of extra defence. York Castle (now Clifford's Tower) had already been rebuilt entirely in stone in the mid-thirteenth century but in 1319 Edward II ordered that it be fortified ready for a siege. The late thirteenth and early fourteenth centuries also saw the city walls (a circuit of 2 miles) strengthened with stone walls and numerous towers. St Mary's Abbey, just outside the city walls, was vulnerable to attack and was,

Clifford's Tower, York. Clifford's Tower is named after Lord Robert Clifford (a rebel with Thomas Earl of Lancaster), who was hanged in chains from the tower in 1322 after Edward II captured him.

St Mary's Abbey, York. When the English royal government came to York, its war capital, the Chancery was housed at the abbey.

therefore, granted a licence to crenellate its precinct wall in 1318.

York also had to accommodate the King, his household and the entire government machinery during their stays between 1298 and 1338. In 1322 twenty-three carts and five horses brought government records from London to York, an undertaking that took thirteen days to complete. Once in York the King, Queen and their households took up residence in the castle, the Franciscan friary or the archbishop's palace. The Chancery was housed in St Mary's Abbey, St Mary's, Castlegate or the Minster Chapter House, and the Exchequer and the King's Bench were located at the castle. New or temporary structures were required at these sites to adapt them for their new roles.

A multangular tower in York city wall. This Roman corner tower was strengthened and heightened in the early fourteenth century to counter the Scottish threat.

Chronicle 'the Scots entered Northumberland in strength, wasting all the land, committing arson, pillage and murder, and advancing almost as far as the town of Newcastle, from which they turned aside and entered the county of Carlisle'. No doubt the harsh weather in Scotland at the time made raids to the south more appealing. Moveable goods were taken and some communities simply had to buy off the Scots. The town at Alnwick was given to the flames, though apparently the castle held out. Newminster Abbey, a Cistercian house, promised gifts to the Scots in return for being spared. Unfortunately, the monks did not fulfil their part of the bargain so the Scots captured the prior and carried away the abbey's goods leaving it empty. Hexham Priory acted as a base for Scottish raids on the surrounding countryside, and some looting also took place at the priory with Wallace's men stealing sacred vessels from the altar. On several occasions Newcastle, at the time not fully enclosed, prepared to be attacked but this did not happen, with Wallace devoting more time to raiding Tynedale (Bywell, Corbridge and Hexham). In Cumberland, Wallace devastated the area from Allerdale to the Derwent at Cockermouth. Carlisle was besieged for a short time but rather more damage was done at Lanercost Priory. The 1297 raids on northern England by Wallace, lasting five weeks, were more severe and extensive than the 1296 raids of the Scottish army at the outset of the war. According to one source, the Scots burned 120 northern vills (townships) in 1296 and 715 vills in 1297. The heaviest damage seems to have been inflicted on northern Northumberland in the settlements in the parishes of Kirk Newton, Norham, Holy Island and Bamburgh, though there was also much damage in the middle Tyne valley.

According to the *Guisborough Chronicle*, an invasion of Durham was contemplated. The fifteenth-century biographer of Wallace, Henry the Minstrel, known as 'Blind Harry', claimed falsely that Wallace penetrated Yorkshire and even captured York:

> Then raised he fire, burn'd Northallerton
> Marched through Yorkshire boldly up and down.
> Destroy'd that land, as far as they could ride
> . . . To York they march, and then they very soon
> With all their force, closely besiege the town.

This exaggeration of Wallace's military campaign should not, however, mask the fact that in 1298 York was actually drawn into war by Edward I. On his return from the Flanders campaign, Edward I reacted to the English defeat at Stirling Bridge by setting up his headquarters at York in the summer of 1298, and ordering the English army to assemble ready to advance into Scotland. This marks the start of the period when York became the war capital for the Scottish Wars. Between 1298 and 1338

York became the administrative capital of England for five periods: 1298–1305, 1319–20, 1322–3, 1327, 1333–8. The Exchequer, the Chancery and the main judicial benches (King's Bench and Common Pleas) were based in York at these times, and Parliament met in York fifteen times during these years. It is difficult to overestimate the wide-ranging impact of all this activity on York as a supply depot for war stores; the presence of purveyors and army contractors all greatly increased the trade and prosperity of the city. The catering industry certainly flourished, as did trades associated with warfare such as saddlers, bowyers, armourers, fletchers and sword-makers. There were clearly opportunities for profiteering by local traders and landlords. Shortly after 1298, the resultant influx of officials, lawyers, suitors and others disrupted local business and forced prices to rise. Complaints reached the Royal Council and as a result, in 1301, a series of lengthy ordinances dealing with prices, weights and measures, hygiene and sanitation were produced. Butchers, for instance, were prohibited from selling 'fresh meat which has lain . . . in the sun . . . for more than one day', and doctors and physicians were not to use 'ripped and bloodstained' bandages. Attempts were made to prevent anyone from keeping pigs 'which go in the street by day and night', or to 'put out excrement or other filth or animal manure in the city'. Undoubtedly, York's transformation into a war capital in 1298 caused a number of problems but this process was also a great stimulus to the city's economy.

The campaign against the Scots was plotted in, and administered from, York. The army that eventually crossed the border in early July 1298 was a large one, boasting 3,000 cavalry and 25,000 infantry. However, everything did not go according to plan – the army was not adequately supplied with food, the Welsh troops (a large proportion of the infantry force) became very drunk and disorderly on a shipment of wine (and empty stomachs), and Edward I was injured by his charger before the battle began. The armies of William Wallace and Edward I eventually met on 22 July just outside Falkirk. Inferior numbers and fear of the English cavalry caused Wallace to adopt a defensive formation on the southern slope of Callendar Wood with the Westquarter Burn just below him. Wallace arranged his troops in four great schiltroms or 'shield walls' comprising between 1,000 and 2,000 spearmen tightly packed into circles. The *Guisborough Chronicle* describes how the front rank of this formation, standing or kneeling, held their spears at an angle of 45 degrees. The impression given by this arrangement was of a hedgehog. The schiltroms were given added protection by wooden stakes driven into the ground at an angle. Wallace realised the need to eliminate horses, probably the weakest feature of the English cavalry. The Scots also had cavalry contributed by the Scottish nobles supporting Wallace and situated in the rear.

The Battle of Falkirk was a hard, closely fought encounter. The Scots succeeded in killing a large number of English horses but in time the

Overleaf:
Caerlaverock Castle. Built by the Maxwells in the thirteenth century, Caerlaverock was 'In shape like a shield' according to a contemporary ballad on the siege. Bruce's forces recaptured it from the English in 1312.

combination of the English long bow (which made its first real mark on a major battle after use in the Welsh campaigns of the 1270s and 1280s) and the weight of the English cavalry proved decisive. The Scottish cavalry, rather ingloriously, fled in panic without putting up any resistance and Wallace and the Scottish nobles with him managed to escape. Wallace's military status, the key to his leadership of the Scottish political community between 1297 and 1298, was destroyed which meant that he lost the leadership of the 'patriot' cause in Scotland. He either resigned or was forced to give up his Guardianship.

The year 1298 was a key stage in Bruce's political career, although it is not clear whether he was actually present at the Battle of Falkirk. The influential nationalist writings of John of Fordun (the *Chronicle of the Scottish Nation*) and Walter Bower (*Scotichronicon*) both held the Scottish nobility responsible for betraying Wallace at Falkirk, in particular the Comyn family. Fordun refers to the 'ill-will, begotten of the spring of envy, which the Comyns had conceived towards the said William', as a result of which 'they, with their accomplices, forsook the field, and escaped unhurt'. Most interestingly, in view of the hero status accorded to Bruce for his later achievements, Fordun also reported: 'It is commonly said that Robert de Bruce – who was afterwards king of Scotland, but then fought on the side of the king of England – was the means of bringing about this victory, for while the Scots stood invincible in their ranks, and could not be broken by either force or stratagem, this Robert Bruce went with one line, under Anthony Bek, by a long road round a hill, and attacked the Scots in the rear.'

Walter Bower in the fifteenth century gives a fuller account portraying Bruce as recognising the error of his ways in supporting Edward and realising his true vocation, i.e. the nationalist cause:

> Pursuing them (Wallace and his men) from the other side, Robert de Bruce, when a steep and impassably deep valley between the troops of the two armies came into view, is said to have called out loudly to William, asking him who it was that drove him to such arrogance as to seek so rashly to fight in opposition to the exalted power of the king of England and of the more powerful section of Scotland. It is said that William replied like this to him: 'Robert, Robert, it is your inactivity and womanish cowardice that spur me to set authority free in your native land. But it is an effeminate man even now, ready as he is to advance from bed to battle, from the shadow into the sunlight, with a pampered body accustomed to a soft life feebly taking up the weight of battle for the liberation of his own country, the burden of the breastplate, it is he who has made me so presumptuous perhaps even foolish and has compelled me to attempt or seize these tasks.' With these words William himself looked to a speedy flight, and with his men sought safety.
>
> On account of all of this Robert himself was like one awakening from a deep sleep, the power of Wallace's words so entered his heart that he no longer had any thought of favouring the views of the English. Hence, as he became every day braver than he had been, he kept all these words uttered by his faithful friend, considering them in his heart.

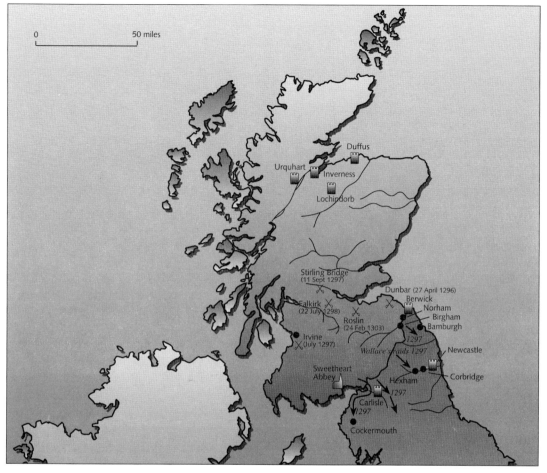

Main events, 1292–1304.

Again, there seems to have been some confusion in the minds of medieval commentators between the actions of Robert Bruce's father and those of his son. It is probable, given his consistent support for the English King, that Robert Bruce senior, the future King's father, was at Falkirk on the English side. It is far from clear that Robert Bruce the younger was on the Scottish side at Falkirk but his actions at about this time – he was in Ayrshire and set fire to the castle at Ayr to prevent its use by the English – would indicate his support for the Scottish cause. What is evident, however, is that William Wallace was regarded with intense suspicion by the traditional Scottish aristocratic leaders including the Bruces and the Comyns. Despite the traditional view that Robert Bruce took over the leadership of the Scottish cause after Wallace's capture and murder in 1305, the reality was very different. The Scottish 'cause' that William Wallace was fighting for was a different one from that promoted

Lochindorb Castle. The importance of this castle is attested by John Comyn II of Badenoch's death there in about 1302 and by Edward I's use of it in 1303 as a base to accept the formal submission of northern Scotland.

by the Bruces. Wallace had consistently campaigned for the kingship of John Balliol; the Bruces had led a civil war against the Balliol kingship in 1286 and 1287 and they put forward their own claims to kingship against Balliol's during the 'Great Cause' of 1291–2. William Wallace fought continually against the English presence in Scotland from his emergence in 1297 as the slayer of the English sheriff at Lanark to his capture and cruel execution in 1305. Robert Bruce, the future King, had started the war in 1296 on the English side opposing a Scottish government trying to uphold John Balliol's kingship as a symbol of Scottish independence. Despite the apparent confluence of interests when the young Bruce came over to the Scottish side in 1297, and seemingly remained there in 1298, Bruce and Wallace had very different interests and causes to fight. The story from Walter Bower of Robert Bruce learning his true vocation from Wallace after the Battle of Falkirk is not borne out by the actions of Bruce between 1298 and Wallace's death in 1305.

Throughout the thirteenth century, the various Scottish political establishments had turned to English kings during political crises in Scotland. Most of the leading Scottish aristocratic families had social, economic and religious interests and obligations in England. The thirteenth century was marked by generally peaceful relations between the two countries and good social bonds between the two royal families. There were a series of marriage alliances between the two families: Alexander II of Scotland's marriage to Joan, daughter of King John, in 1221, Alexander III of Scotland's marriage to Margaret, daughter of Henry III, in 1251 and the preliminary marriage arrangements made to join the Maid of Norway with Edward I's son in 1290. These unions helped to encourage a social interaction between leading noble families in Scotland and the English Court. This meant that it was quite natural for the majority of Scottish nobility, especially those with particular English interests, to approach the English King as a 'friendly' and militarily stronger neighbour to promote their interests within Scotland. This was a concept alien to Wallace though not to the Bruces, who wanted support for their own royal claims in Scotland, or the Comyns who wanted to see their dominance of the political scene in Scotland continued under the Balliol kingship.

Unlike the Bruces, the Comyns' animosity to Wallace was based on the fact that their long-held leadership of the Scottish political community had been lost to Wallace between 1296 and 1297 during their imprisonment in England. As already noted, the Comyns were blamed by Fordun and Bower for treacherously forsaking Wallace at Falkirk, which, of course, reflects the need for the nationalist narratives of Fordun and Bower to condemn any rivals to their 'national heroes'. Wallace's actions in power do, however, intimate that a personal animosity existed at the time. Wallace is thought to have attacked the Comyns' interests in Galloway. He also ensured that the Comyns did not appoint their own candidate to the premier bishopric in Scotland, the bishopric of St Andrews, vacant after the death of William Fraser in France in 1297. Comyn domination of Scottish politics in the second half of the thirteenth century had been enhanced by a line of pro-Comyn Bishops of St Andrews: Gamelin (1255–71), probably a relative, and William Wishart (1271–9) and William Fraser (1279–97), who also had Comyn associations. It seems that the Comyns had another family candidate in line for this post, the highest ecclesiastical office in Scotland and also a position of great political significance. Master William Comyn, Provost of St Andrews (1287–1329) and brother of John Comyn, Earl of Buchan, objected to his exclusion from the election process in 1297. Later, in 1306, it was asserted that he had, in fact, been elected Bishop of St Andrews but superseded by William Lamberton, Wallace's candidate. This allegation, if correct, would certainly explain the hostility between the Comyns and Lamberton after 1298.

Although Fordun and Bower made much of Wallace's betrayal by both Bruce and Comyn at Falkirk, this was not an issue at the time, which is illustrated by the political community's immediate acceptance of John Comyn, the younger, of Badenoch as Guardian of Scotland following Wallace's resignation. The Comyns' long-held leadership of the Scottish political community had been interrupted by their absence in England from 1296 to 1297 and their position would no longer be unquestioned. The new Guardianship of 1298 was a joint one between John Comyn, the younger, and Robert Bruce, Earl of Carrick (the future king) – Bruce, and indeed the Bruce family, had gained national political power for the first time. Bruce, as well as Wallace, had benefited from the Comyns' absence and Bruce himself had gained a much higher political profile despite his poor military showing in 1297. The joint Guardianship was an unlikely alliance given the hostility between Bruces and Comyns since 1286. It was seen at the time as a compromise, forming a government of national unity in which the military resources and patronage of the two most influential families in Scotland could be used to secure the continued independence of the Scottish kingdom. After Falkirk, it appeared that Robert Bruce was prepared, after his family's long and bitter struggle against John Balliol's kingship, to act on behalf of the absent John Balliol, who was still held hostage in England.

That the tensions between Comyn and Bruce were only just below the surface became apparent at a council of magnates in Peebles on 19 August 1299. A quarrel developed between David Graham, a firm Comyn adherent, and Malcolm Wallace, William Wallace's brother. Graham put forward a 'demand for William Wallace's lands and goods as he was going abroad without leave – after resigning the Guardianship, Wallace continued to work on behalf of John Balliol's kingship at the French and papal courts until returning to Scotland in 1303. Graham's request met strong objections from Malcolm Wallace. During the argument, John Comyn, the younger, 'leapt at the earl of Carrick and seized him by the throat, and the earl of Buchan turned on the bishop of St Andrews [Lamberton]'. A compromise was reached in which William Lamberton, no doubt in his role as Bishop of St Andrews, became a third Guardian acting as a buffer between the two secular leaders. By 1300 it had become clear, however, that John Comyn found it as difficult to work with Lamberton as he did with Bruce. At a parliament held at Rutherglen in May 1300, the more Comyn-orientated Ingram de Umphraville, a kinsman of Balliol and a Comyn ally, was brought in to replace Robert Bruce as one of the Guardians. Bruce may have resigned at this parliament or just before.

A number of reasons have been put forward to explain the resignation or replacement of Bruce as Guardian. Bruce may have objected to the fact that the military activity in the Anglo-Scottish War was concentrated in the south-west in 1300, after Edward led an army into Galloway in the summer of that year. At this time most of the Bruce lands, which were concentrated in the south-west, were in English hands. Bruce had tried to regain Lochmaben and Annan in 1299 after the Peebles meeting in August but Lochmaben was still held by the English under Robert Felton in 1300. The capture of the fine Scottish-held castle of Caerlaverock further strengthened the English position in the south-west. It was, in fact, the English highlight of the campaign, as the *Lanercost Chronicle* recorded: 'The King did nothing remarkable this time against the Scots whose land he entered, because they always fled before him, skulking in moors and woods, wherefore his army was taken back to England.' Political problems and distractions had prevented Edward I from following up the Falkirk campaign and, therefore, that English victory did not prove as decisive as it initially appeared to be. The Scots had regrouped and learned the lesson of Falkirk – avoid large pitched battles against the superior weight of the English cavalry. This was a lesson learnt by Robert Bruce as well as the other Scottish leaders. During his time as Guardian, Bruce had taken part in a number of military actions. In November 1299 he was with Comyn and Lamberton at Torwood waiting for the English garrison of Stirling to surrender. He also joined in a full-scale raid south of the Forth which, originally, intended to attack Roxburgh until caution (the result of Falkirk) again came to the fore.

It was only partly due to the reality of English occupation of Bruce lands and castles in the south-west that Bruce withdrew from the Guardianship in 1300. It also seemed probable that the diplomatic efforts of William Wallace, Matthew Crambeth, Bishop of Dunkeld, and others at the courts of the French King and the papacy would lead to a return to Scotland of John Balliol. He had been released by the English into papal custody in 1299 and in the summer of 1301, as a result of diplomatic pressure applied to the French and in turn French pressure on the Pope, Balliol was returned to his family lands in Picardy. There was optimism in Scotland that, with French support, Balliol could soon return to Scotland. The Truce of Asnières, negotiated in France and ratified by King Philip, granted a truce to the Scots in the war with England to last from 26 January to 1 November 1302. According to the terms, the French were to hold certain lands in the south-west during the truce – these lands would probably include the Earl of Carrick's castle at Turnberry (Turnberry had fallen to the English in September 1301) as well as the Bruces' Annandale lands. The probability of Balliol's return to Scotland must have made Robert Bruce's position in Scotland increasingly untenable. Bruce's father (and grandfather) had never sworn fealty to Balliol and the Bruces had been in active opposition to Balliol since 1286. It must have been galling for young Robert Bruce as Guardian between 1298 and 1300 to have to attach his seal to government acts as one of 'Guardians of the kingdom of Scotland in the name of the famous prince the lord John, by God's grace illustrious king of Scotland, appointed by the community of that realm'. That may have been bearable when Balliol was an 'absentee king' but difficult for any member of the Bruce family to tolerate with Balliol back in Scotland. The renewal of Bruce's alliance with Edward I by February 1302 was a logical next step after his resignation/replacement as Guardian.

Robert Bruce was one of the first major nobles to desert the 'national' cause. His loyalty to Edward I was consolidated by a marriage alliance, a strategy previously employed by the English King to try to control the Stewarts, Balliols and Comyns. Bruce took, as his second wife, Elizabeth, daughter of Richard de Burgh, Earl of Ulster. The terms of Bruce's submission to Edward I have been the subject of much debate and interpretation because of their vagueness. It seems that Bruce wanted Edward I's support for the Bruce landed rights in Scotland as well as the family's claim to the Scottish throne: 'Because Robert [?] fears that the [?] realm of Scotland might be removed from the hands of the king, which God forbid, and delivered to John Balliol, or to his son, or that the right might be put in question, or reversed and appealed in a new judgement, the king grants to Robert that he may pursue his right and the king will hear him fairly and hold him to justice in the king's court' (printed in E.L.G. Stones (ed.), *Anglo-Scottish Relations, 1174–1328*). The imminence of Balliol's return to Scotland brought yet more changes to the membership of the Scottish Guardianship. The triumvirate of Comyn, Lamberton and Umphraville lasted until 1301 (certainly no later than May). At about this time it seems they were superseded by John de Soules, appointed by John Balliol directly as his agent in Scotland pending his return. It is probable, however, that he was an additional voice in the Scottish leadership as John Comyn was sole Guardian in Scotland from the autumn of 1302, when Soules went to Paris on a diplomatic mission.

The Scottish war effort continued quite successfully without Bruce's leadership after his defection and alliance with Edward I. Though Bruce had resigned from the Guardianship by May 1300, his support for the Scottish cause seems to be implied by the presence of the 'army of Carrick', which remained at the disposal of Soules and the Scottish patriots late in 1301. The Scots still tended to avoid major battles but John Comyn, described as 'leader and captain' of the Scottish army, won a notable victory on 24 February 1303 when, with Simon Fraser, he defeated the English at Roslin (Midlothian). This success was acknowledged by the Scots in Paris in a letter to Comyn: 'it would gladden your heart if you would know how much your honour has increased in every part of the world as the result of your recent victory with the English [Roslin]'.

Edward I's response was to launch, in 1303, the first English campaign to northern Scotland since 1296. The campaign concentrated on the heart of Comyn power, i.e. north-east Scotland, taking Aberdeen and Banff. Edward also acquired the Comyn castles of Lochindorb and Balvenie and there was little resistance to his progress. Lochindorb, symbolically, as the chief private castle of the Comyn Lords of Badenoch (the senior line of the Comyn family), was used by Edward I as a base to receive the submission of the north. John Comyn the younger, of Badenoch, recognised both politically and militarily as leader of the Scottish community of the realm from 1302 to 1304, led the negotiations for the wholesale Scottish submission in January and February 1304. The major English campaign of 1303 had coincided with the loss of Scotland's main ally, France, by May 1303. The French army had been defeated by a Flemish force at Courtrai on 11 July 1302 and the Anglo-French peace treaty that followed, on 20 May 1303, excluded the Scots despite the diplomatic efforts of John de Soules, William Lamberton and John Comyn, Earl of Buchan. These factors, as well as the steady flow of significant Scottish support to Edward I – the Macdougalls (Comyn allies) in 1301, Robert Bruce, by February 1302, Alexander de Abernethy (also a Comyn ally) in 1302 and William, Earl of Ross (another Comyn supporter), in September 1303 – led John Comyn to try to negotiate the best possible terms from a position of relative military strength. There had been no major military defeat for the Scottish army in 1303.

There is no doubt that John Comyn was speaking as leader of the Scottish political community in 1304; he was acting for the Scottish delegation at the French Court as well as those in Scotland. The language he used was that of a 'patriot' leader not a puppet. It should be pointed out, however, that William Wallace, John de Soules and Simon Fraser did not submit to Edward I in 1304. Wallace had returned to Scotland in 1303 and in June of that year he, in the company of Fraser and Comyn, had attacked Robert Bruce's home territory of Annandale. In February 1304, Bruce was with the English army who tried to seize Wallace and Fraser near Peebles. Wallace and Bruce had their differences: Wallace was a consistent supporter of the Balliol kingship; Robert Bruce certainly was not. The military conflict between Wallace, still representing Balliol, and Bruce, representing Edward I in 1303 and 1304, emphasises the gulf between the two men.

When John Comyn negotiated for the general Scottish submission in February 1304, Robert Bruce had been an ally of Edward I since February 1302 at the latest. He was an active participant in Edward I's summer campaign of 1303 and the King seemed to value Robert Bruce's support as he made him Sheriff of Lanark and Ayr. Edward Bruce, Robert's younger brother, served in the entourage of Edward, Prince of Wales. Robert Bruce, by sending siege weapons, made a contribution to the capture of Stirling in July 1304, the successful conclusion of which set the seal on the English military victory in 1304. Robert Bruce seemed set for reward in Scotland as a valued ally of Edward I.

BRUCE'S COUP
AND THE DEATH OF
COMYN THE RED

T he years 1304 to 1306 saw Robert Bruce move rapidly and dramatically from being the ally of Edward I to being the murderer of John Comyn, leader of the political community of Scotland (10 February 1306), and six weeks afterwards to acquiring the kingship of Scotland, a prize his family had long sought. It is natural to link the capture and violent execution of William Wallace (August 1305) with Bruce's decision to seize the crown and carry on Wallace's 'heroic' work. It has been seen, however, that there was no natural affinity between Wallace and Bruce. Wallace's execution certainly raised the political temperature among the leaders of the Scottish political community at the time but the seeds of the Bruce 'coup' were already being sown in 1304.

As has been noted previously, Robert Bruce the future King was very much a product of his family background and was greatly influenced by his family's political ambitions, especially those of his grandfather. Robert Bruce, the Competitor, who had died in 1295, was described by the *Lanercost Chronicle* as 'a noble man of England as well as of Scotland, heir of Annandale [who] departed from this world, aged and full of days. He was of handsome appearance, a gifted speaker, remarkable for his influence.' The future King's grandfather probably influenced him more than his father had done but there is no doubt that his father's death on 21 April 1304 radically changed Bruce's personal circumstances. Now aged thirty, Robert Bruce owned the lordship of Annandale as well as the earldom of Carrick and part of Garioch (Aberdeenshire). He was acting guardian for his young neighbour in the north, Donald, Earl of Mar (and nephew by marriage), and thus exercised more influence in northern Scotland than ever before. With his father's death, Bruce had inherited his family's claim to the Scottish throne, which his grandfather had skilfully passed on to his successors before a final judgement was made in favour of John Balliol. This claim had been a strong factor affecting the internal politics of Scotland after the death of Alexander III in 1286. Robert Bruce, twelve years of age in 1286, must have been very conscious of his grandfather's determination to pursue the family's

Seal of Robert Bruce, Earl of Carrick (d. 1304), the father of the future king, depicted on the obverse of the seal (*c.* 1285) in chain mail, surcoat, helmet with grated visor and a sword in his right hand. By permission of the Court of the Lord Lyon.

claim after 1286. Bruce inherited his family's claim and ambitions at a very fortuitous time – the submission negotiated by John Comyn in February 1304 dealt a great blow to the revival of John Balliol's kingship; it was also known that Edward I was ill and not expected to live long.

Although the Scottish kingdom developed a mature and sophisticated government in the second half of the thirteenth century with a clear idea of its own identity, laws, customs and independence, there was a pragmatic common sense displayed by political groups in Scotland in their awareness of the greater military power and influence of their neighbour, England. Both Comyns and Bruces had consistently appealed for English help during political troubles in Scotland since 1286. Robert Bruce's actions in the period 1304 to 1306 must, therefore, be placed in the context of Edward I's plans for Scotland after the 1304 submission, and also his plans for Bruce himself. Edward seems to have learnt from some of the mistakes made in 1296 over his management of Scotland after Dunbar. He had already started to appoint more Scots to his administration as he gradually won more control in 1303 and 1304. He rewarded, for instance, those Scots such as Alexander de Abernethy; John, Earl of Atholl; William, Earl of Ross and Robert Bruce, who had all submitted to him before 1304. Bruce was made Sheriff of Ayr and Lanark in 1303,

Overleaf:
Kildrummy Castle, one of the largest baronial castles of thirteenth-century Scotland. Robert Bruce held it by 1305 as the guardian of the Earl of Mar.

a role he retained in 1304. Further, Edward I used Robert Bruce with Robert Wishart, Bishop of Glasgow, and John de Mowbray as his Scottish advisers during the consultation process before the final settlement for the governance of Scotland was agreed, the Ordinances of September 1305.

After the dust had settled and Edward I's arrangements for the new constitution of Scotland were known through the Ordinances, Robert Bruce must have been very disappointed at how small a role he had in the governing of Scotland. Following the recommendation of the three Scottish advisers, ten representatives were to be elected by the Scottish community of the realm to act as advisers to the English parliament in framing the Ordinances – Robert Bruce was not one of the ten. According to the 1305 Ordinances, Bruce held no position of responsibility in Scotland and he had even lost the sheriffdoms of Ayr and Lanark, which he had held until 1304. The only body in which Bruce is named is the council of twenty-one Scots, an advisory council to the new lieutenant of Scotland, John of Brittany. This was a list dominated by the Comyns and their associates and seems to reflect those whom Edward I viewed as comprising the political community of the realm. The Ordinances of 1305 not only seem to diminish Bruce's hopes and ambitions, they also seem to reflect some lack of trust in Bruce's loyalty: 'Further it is agreed that the earl of Carrick be ordered to put the castle of Kildrummy in the keeping of a man for whom he is willing to answer.' Compared to other Scottish nobles who had surrendered before the general Scottish submission of 1304, including some who had submitted after Bruce's agreement with Edward I, e.g. John, Earl of Atholl, William, Earl of Ross and Alexander de Abernethy, Robert Bruce seems to have been given less responsibility and very little, if any, reward for the military support he gave Edward I. He was not even rewarded with land for his allegiance in war since early 1302.

This treatment of Robert Bruce in 1305 may reflect some suspicion surrounding Bruce's actions in 1304. This concern would certainly have been warranted. Bruce was making his own plans as early as 11 June 1304 when he drew up a secret bond with William Lamberton, Bishop of St Andrews, promising 'to be of one another's counsel in all their business and affairs at all times and against whichever individuals'. This pact must be placed into the context of unrest following the submission of February 1304. Certain individuals were very slow to submit – James Stewart, Simon Fraser and Ingram de Umphraville had not submitted by 12 April; William Wallace and John de Soules refused to submit; Stirling Castle was not captured by the English until July 1304. A number of Scottish nobles had grievances during the course of the years 1304 and 1305. James Stewart, for example, did not get his lands back until November 1305. Simon Fraser submitted late, perhaps as late as 1305, and was punished with a long exile as well as paying three year's value of his lands for their restoration to him. In most cases the threat of exile as punishment for those who submitted to

Edward I was remitted in favour of a money fine. Bishop Robert Wishart of Glasgow was also punished more harshly than others in the surrender terms of 1304. Edward's impatience with the lingering resistance to him after February 1304 caused him to issue a challenge, on the day after the siege of Stirling was over, to the leading nobles of Scotland to prove their loyalty to him in very practical terms. They were told 'to make an effort between now and 13 January 1305 to take Sir William Wallace and hand him over to the king so that he can see how each one bears himself whereby he can have better regard towards the one who takes him'.

This atmosphere of unrest evident in 1304 seems to be confirmed by signs of other plotting. When Wallace was eventually captured in August 1305, documents were found in his possession linking him in 'confederations' with unspecified Scottish nobles. It is not known if Bruce was involved in this too, though it is possible given Wallace's known links with Lamberton. It is clear, however, that Bruce was seeking wider support. The weakness of the Bruces' position and their claims to power since 1286 was due to an insufficiently wide power base. An alliance with Lamberton certainly broadened his support. It could be said that Wallace was too much in favour of Balliol as King to rally behind Bruce while Balliol was still alive. Bruce, however, seems to have been casting for support wherever he could find it. Any conspiracy in 1304 would have had to take into account the power of the Comyns, the force behind the Balliol kingship. The Comyns' position had not collapsed with the submission of 1304 – they had lost political power at the centre of Scottish government though they retained their vast landed influence on payment of a fine and also retained much political authority in the localities through their network of associates whom Edward I sought to employ to control northern Scotland.

According to tradition established by nationalist writers of the fourteenth and fifteenth centuries,

Seal of Marjorie Bruce, Countess of Carrick, and mother of the future king. The pointed oval seal (*c.* 1285) depicts a shield of arms (those of her husband), which is suspended from a tree. By permission of the Court of the Lord Lyon.

WILLIAM WALLACE, A HERO IN DEFEAT

Sometime in May 1297, William Wallace emerged from relative obscurity – he was from a knightly family in the following of James Stewart – to a position at the forefront of Scottish politics by murdering William Heselrig the English Sheriff of Lanark. Whether this was occasioned by Heselrig's murder of Marion Braidfute, Wallace's wife or mistress (according to the traditional account) is not known for certain. What is clear is that Wallace had considerable military ability, as displayed on 11 September 1297 when, with Andrew Moray, he led the Scots to victory against an English force at Stirling Bridge. Following this victory, large parts of Northumberland and Cumberland felt the destructive impact of Wallace and his army; in particular, Newcastle and Carlisle were threatened.

The Wallace monument, Stirling. Completed in 1869, near his great triumph at Stirling Bridge, the monument contains a bronze statue of Wallace in chain mail holding aloft his huge sword.

Newcastle town walls. Little remains of the 2-mile circuit (started in 1265) praised for its 'strength and magnificence' in the sixteenth century. Wallace's raid in 1297 speeded up its completion.

Alnwick Castle. Heavily fortified under the Percies in the fourteenth century, Alnwick Castle was still strong enough in 1297 to resist William Wallace, who lacked siege weaponry. In a strategically important position guarding the main route north across the River Aln, the castle was sold to Henry de Percy by the Bishop of Durham in 1309.

English writers portray William Wallace as the 'leader of these savages', 'a robber' and an 'unworthy man'. In Scottish tradition, however, Wallace became the first popular leader of Scottish nationalism. To John of Fordun, who wrote in the 1380s, Wallace was 'wondrously brave and bold, of goodly mien, and boundless liberality'. Henry the Minstrel (Blind Harry) added much fiction to Wallace's achievement in his vernacular poem *The Wallace* (composed in the 1470s). *The Wallace* remains the most important source behind all subsequent histories of Wallace and film adaptations such as *Braveheart*. Despite defeat at Falkirk in 1298, Wallace was 'a man who never submitted to the English' (Walter Bower). His savage execution by the English in 1305 ensured that he became the martyr for the cause of Scottish nationalism.

Cockermouth Castle. Following his success at Stirling Bridge in 1297, Wallace raided northern England. In Cumberland his attacks devastated the area from Allerdale to the Derwent at Cockermouth.

Bruce approached John Comyn of Badenoch with a 'kind-hearted plan' to end 'the endless tormenting of the people'. Robert gave Comyn the choice of two courses of action: either Comyn should reign, with Bruce gaining all of Comyn's lands or Bruce should become king, with all of Bruce's lands going to Comyn. According to Fordun (the *Chronicle of Scottish Nation*), Comyn preferred the latter option and a solemn covenant was made between them but 'John broke his word, and heedless of the sacredness of his oath, kept accusing Robert before the king of England, through his ambassadors and private letters, and wickedly revealing that Robert's secrets.' This forms the background, according to the pro-Bruce Scottish tradition, to the infamous murder of John Comyn by Robert Bruce in the Greyfriars Church at Dumfries on 10 February 1306. After being confronted with his treachery at their meeting in the church, 'the evil-speaker is stabbed and wounded unto death'. According to both Scottish and English traditions, John Comyn was killed in two stages, with Bruce's men going back to the church to finish the deed. The fifteenth-century chronicler Walter Bower recorded that Bruce had returned to Lochmaben Castle after the stabbing and reported to his kinsmen, James Lindsay and Roger Kilpatrick, 'I think I have killed John the Red Comyn'. Bruce's men returned to the church, with Roger Kilpatrick, according to a wholly fabulous tale, exclaiming 'I mak siccar.'

The murder of John Comyn, acknowledged by both Scots and English as the most powerful man in the country, was such a dramatic and important event in Scottish history, as well as in Robert Bruce's career, that strong Scottish and English traditions developed about it. Scottish traditions emphasised Comyn's treachery, while English tradition emphasised that the murder was premeditated. The contemporary report of Walter of Guisborough deserves some precedence. According to Guisborough, Bruce feared that Comyn would hinder him in his attempt to gain the Scottish throne and sent two of his brothers, Thomas and Neil, from his castle at Lochmaben to Comyn's castle at Dalswinton, 10 miles away, asking Comyn to meet him at the Greyfriars Church at Dumfries to discuss 'certain business'. This seems likely to have been related to the 'agreement' they may have made in 1304, perhaps a general compact similar to the one made with Lamberton rather that the specific one mentioned by nationalist writers. The business, no doubt, involved Bruce's desire to revive Scottish kingship with Bruce on the throne. After initially friendly words, a sign perhaps of an earlier understanding between the two men, Bruce turned on Comyn and accused him of treacherously reporting to Edward I that he (Bruce) was plotting against him. It seems most probable that their bitter antagonisms of the past – they had, literally, come to blows at a baronial council at Peebles in 1299 – were instantly revived and, in a heated argument, mutual charges of treachery were made. It is unlikely that the murder was premeditated. Bruce struck Comyn with a dagger and his men attacked him with swords.

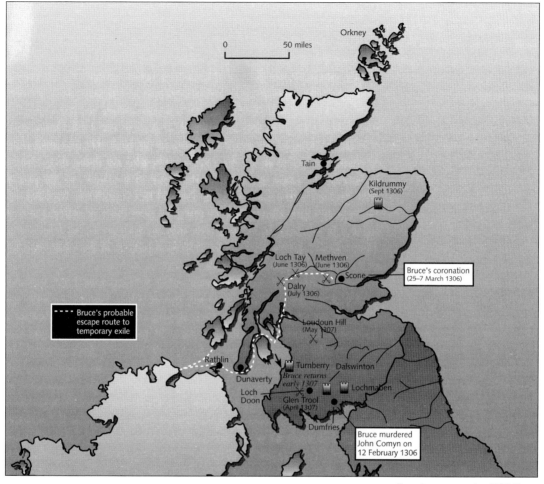

Bruce's movements, 1304–7.

Comyn's uncle, Robert, was killed by Christopher Seton when he attempted to defend his nephew. According to both English and Scottish tradition, Comyn himself was mortally wounded, left for dead and finally killed later.

In the circumstances of Anglo-Scottish politics at the time, it is most probable that the argument was less about 'nationalism' and 'treachery' and more about having the ear of the English king and his influence and backing. Undoubtedly, the Comyns had this in 1306. Edward I reported to the Pope that Robert Bruce had risen against him as a 'traitor' and 'murdered Sir John Comyn, lord of Badenoch in the church of the Friars Minor of the town of Dumfries, by the high altar, because Sir John would not assent to the treason which Robert planned to perpetrate against the king of England, namely, to resume war against him and make himself king of Scotland'. Bruce's great disappointment at the outcome of his alliance with Edward I since 1302 must be contrasted with the Comyns' position. They had led Scottish resistance to Edward I in 1296 and, after their imprisonment in England from 1296 to 1297, also in and after 1298. Considering their desertion of Edward I in 1297, the Comyns were treated very leniently in the submission terms, more tolerantly than several others on the 'patriot' side such as James Stewart, Simon Fraser, William Wallace and Robert Wishart, Bishop of Glasgow. The Comyns were confirmed in their vast landed heritage merely on payment of a fine. Edward I's main aim in Scotland, as seen in the 1305 Ordinances, was 'the keeping of the peace and quiet of the land'. He described John Comyn's murder as an act 'by some people who are doing their utmost to trouble the peace and quiet of the realm of Scotland'. In the period after Alexander III's death in 1286, Edward had consistently regarded the Comyns and their associates as the grouping most likely to deliver political stability in Scotland. In keeping with this, the leniency to the Comyns in 1304 reflected Edwards's need for their tacit support in the administration of Scotland, especially in the north.

John Comyn had come to terms with Edward I in 1304 without suffering military defeat, without the family's extensive range of castles being slighted or their lands destroyed. He probably felt that a military campaign against the full force of Edward I's army could not be successful without considerable support from the French King. As a practical and pragmatic politician, John Comyn, 'perceiving that he could not withstand the might of the King of England', realised that the Comyns had more to lose than any other family in Scotland from full-scale war with England. If he had ambitions to renew the struggle for John Balliol's kingship, the time was not yet right. The Comyns may well have thought that Edward I would eventually restore them to their former power at the centre of Scottish politics, and they had no incentive to go along with Bruce's plans.

The new Scottish constitution of 1305 could be said to fulfil key aspects of Comyn's submission demands in 1304 – the recognition that the laws, customs, usages and franchises were to be retained as they had been in Alexander III's reign and that amendments would only be made with the advice of the 'good men' of Scotland seemed to affirm Scotland's rights. However, it is clear from the Ordinances that Edward I no longer regarded Scotland as a kingdom; it was consistently referred to in the Ordinances as 'the land of Scotland'. It would have a similar status, in Edward's eyes, to that of Wales and Ireland. Given the tensions in Scotland and the pacts already being made in 1304, Edward's decision to abolish the kingdom must have raised the political temperature in Scotland even further. The capture and savage execution of Wallace in August 1305 also inflamed the situation. It formed an important background event to the Bruce coup of 1306 but it is debatable whether it inspired Bruce to that act in quite the manner represented in Scottish tradition.

The capture and execution of William Wallace in 1305 removed perhaps the foremost supporter of the Balliol cause. It is possible that Bruce was involved in Wallace's capture. That notion should not be ruled out – Bruce had been actively involved in the hunt for Wallace when fighting for Edward I in 1303 and 1304. It was John of Menteith who captured Wallace eventually and later Menteith became an associate of Bruce. There is no definite proof that Bruce was involved in Wallace's capture but there is also no record of Bruce protesting against, or trying to prevent, Wallace's execution. Their causes were very different and Wallace's removal made it much easier, in practice, to resurrect the Bruce claim to the throne. In 1306, however, Robert Bruce did not have general support in Scotland for his ambitions; he did not yet represent the community of the realm of Scotland, and John Balliol was not dead. There was a need for Bruce either to come to some arrangement with the Comyns, the power behind the Balliol kingship – to win their support or at least their neutrality – or to destroy their power. The murder of John Comyn at the Greyfriars Church on 10 February 1306 meant that Bruce's ambitions depended on the destruction of the Comyn power bases in Scotland.

The fact that Robert Bruce was enthroned King of Scots only six weeks after the murder reveals that some preliminary planning had been carried

Auchen/Auchencass Castle. A thirteenth-century baronial stronghold, Auchen (Dumfriesshire) was prized by both Robert Bruce and Edward I.

out. The murder undoubtedly accelerated plans that Bruce was already preparing with William Lamberton, Bishop of St Andrews, and Robert Wishart, Bishop of Glasgow. The ceremony itself took place, symbolically, at Scone Abbey, although the Stone of Destiny was missing, still being held at Westminster Abbey. Though Scottish tradition tends to place greater emphasis on Bruce's war against the English and eventual triumph at the Battle of Bannockburn in 1314, the reality in 1306 was that a full-scale civil war, always threatened since 1286, had broken out in Scotland. Robert Bruce would have to assert his control over Scotland before he could acquire enough military resources to fight the English. According to John of Fordun, 'not only did he [Bruce] lift his hand against the king of England . . . but he also launched out into a struggle with all and sundry of the kingdom of Scotland, except a few well-wishers of his, who, if one looked at the hosts of those pitted against them, were as one drop of water compared with the waves of the sea or a single grain of any seed with the multitudinous sand'. No doubt, Fordun understated Bruce's support in 1306 to heighten his hero's eventual triumph but, in truth, he had formidable obstacles to overcome before he could be accepted as King in Scotland.

At the coronation ceremony at Scone in 1306, Robert Bruce was supported by the earls of Lennox, Atholl, Menteith and possibly the young Earl of Mar (who was in Bruce's guardianship at the time). The traditional role in the ceremony conducted by the Earl of Fife was taken by his aunt, Isabel, wife of John Comyn, Earl of Buchan. This was a notable early desertion from the Comyn cause. Bishops in support of Bruce at his coronation were the bishops of St Andrews (Lamberton), Glasgow (Wishart) – Wishart 'gave him absolution fully for his sins' – Dunkeld and Moray. Very few of those placed in positions of authority by the 1305 Ordinances supported Bruce in 1306. Of the seventeen sheriffs named in the Ordinances, only three (Walter Barclay, William Mowat and Malcolm Innerpeffry) joined Bruce in 1306. As in 1286, Bruce's first military activity was in the south-west where the traditional Bruce strength in land and castles was consolidated by the taking of the Comyn castle of Dalswinton, the Siward castle of Tibbers and the royal castles of Dumfries and Ayr. Bruce was unable, however, to win over the people of Galloway (long under the influence of Comyns and Balliols) to his cause. Bruce's own castle at Loch Doon and one he had recently acquired, Dunaverty, were stocked up with victuals as his allies first took Rothesay Castle and then besieged Inverkip (Renfrew). Bruce's strength had traditionally been in the south-west and this provided convenient access to Irish allies. Bruce's support was already beginning to widen beyond the south-west. He travelled to Glasgow and Rutherglen and then to Aberdeen and probably Banff to gain support in the north. Associates were sent to capture Brechin and Cupar, while Bruce himself gained Dundee town. Damage was done to the castles of Forfar, Aboyne and Aberdeen. The gradual widening of support for Bruce may have been due to the number of individuals and families who were dissatisfied with either English overlordship or the settlement of 1305. Edward I was, himself, to acknowledge in 1307 that his Ordinances (1305) may have been 'too harsh and rigorous'.

Despite some early increase in his support, the weight of support in Scotland was clearly on the side of the Comyns and their associates. The Comyn party were soon roused to action with John Comyn, Earl of Buchan, the new leader of the Comyn party, John de Mowbray, Alexander de Abernethy, Ingram de Umphraville, Edmund Comyn of Kilbride, Richard Siward, William de Balliol, Adam Gordon and David, son of the Earl of Atholl, all prominent. Family endorsement from William, Earl of Ross, and Alexander Macdougall, Lord of Argyll, was apparent later in the year. English support came swiftly to the Comyn cause. By 5 April 1306, Edward I had appointed Aymer de Valence, Comyn's brother-in-law, as his special lieutenant in Scotland with wide-ranging powers against Bruce. Henry de Percy was given similar responsibilities in the west. Edward I's special links with the Comyns are emphasised in a number of ways. Edward ordered Joan de Valence, his cousin, to send her son, John, the murdered John Comyn's son and heir, to England where he was to be in the care of Sir John Weston, master and guardian of the royal children. This was not the only marriage that linked the Comyns with important members of the English nobility. Alexander Comyn of Buchan, who was Sheriff of Aberdeen for Edward I between 1297 and 1304 (slightly out of step with the family in this period), had married Joan, sister of William Latimer, a prominent force in the English military campaigns against Scotland. In addition, Alice, niece and co-heiress of John Comyn, Earl of Buchan, had married Henry Beaumont, another well-established English noble.

The Comyns and their associates had a dominant position in the north where the resources and castles of the earldoms of Buchan, Ross and Sutherland and the strategically important lordships of Badenoch, Lochaber and Argyll were formidable. When these assets in the north were linked with the combined strength of English resources and the Comyn party in southern and south-western Scotland, Robert Bruce's task became incredibly difficult. It is hardly surprising that the combined Comyn–English forces achieved early successes. Bishop Lamberton, who had apparently made overtures for surrender in June 1306, was arrested together with Bishop Wishart and imprisoned in southern England.

The first military setback for Bruce occurred at the Battle of Methven near Perth on 19 June 1306. In command of the English army (300 cavalry and 2,000 infantry) was Aymer de Valence, with the Comyn supporters John de Mowbray, Ingram de Umphraville and Alexander de Abernethy in his following. This force recaptured Cupar and the walled city of Perth. Bruce's army was caught scattered and unprepared near Perth at Methven and, although there was hard fighting, it was more of a rout than a battle.

Overleaf:
Ben Lawers and Loch Tay. Robert Bruce suffered defeat beside Loch Tay immediately after his defeat at Methven (near Perth). He hurried westward to seek refuge.

Bruce was lucky to escape with his light cavalry but a few days later apparently suffered another defeat beside Loch Tay. The new Scottish King was forced to flee westwards and lurk with his men in the borders of Atholl and Argyll but in late July he suffered another military setback at Dalry, 1 mile south-east of Tyndrum (Perthshire). He was defeated here by John Macdougall of Argyll, a Comyn relative and ally, and his followers. From this point it seemed that Bruce's military organisation, such as it was, disintegrated and his following fled to safety. His wife and daughter, Marjory, were taken to Kildrummy Castle as a safe haven by the Earl of Atholl. Kildrummy Castle, on Donside, was in the charge of Robert Bruce's brother, Neil, but early in September it fell to Aymer de Valence as a result of treachery within the castle. Before the fall of Kildrummy, the royal ladies had been sent north in the charge of the Earl of Atholl. It is thought that they were on their way to Orkney because of the Bruces' close connections with the Norwegian royal family. The party was intercepted at Tain by the pro-Comyn Earl of Ross.

The English could not find Robert Bruce but they took a large number of castles and also many prisoners. What followed could only be described as cruel repression, revenge for Bruce's murder of John Comyn and the Bruce family suffered immensely. His brother, Neil, captured at Kildrummy, was hung, drawn and then executed at Berwick. His sister, Mary, was imprisoned in a cage placed in a tower at Roxburgh Castle. The Countess of Buchan, Isabel, who had betrayed her husband, John Comyn, Earl of Buchan, and had participated in the crowning of Bruce, was placed in a similar construction at Berwick, where an English source described the cage as a 'little house of timber . . . the sides latticed so that all there could gaze on her as a spectacle'. The inspiration for this somewhat bizarre form of punishment appears to have originated in Italy. Bruce's wife, by comparison, was placed in honourable captivity in Holderness apparently saved from punishment by the allegiance of her father, the Earl of Ulster, to Edward. Bruce's young daughter, Marjory, was sent to a Yorkshire nunnery and another sister, Christian, wife of Christopher Seton, was kept in a Lincolnshire nunnery. Her husband, Christopher, did not escape so lightly. He had taken part in the murder of John Comyn and, after being taken at the Bruce castle of Loch Doon, was punished like other serious offenders. He was hung, drawn and executed at Dumfries, an ironic end for one who had helped murder John Comyn in that town. Christopher's brother, John, was captured at Tibbers Castle and taken to Newcastle, where he too was drawn and hanged. Key Bruce adherents, Simon Fraser and John, Earl of Atholl, were taken to London for execution. Simon Fraser, because of his treachery to Edward I, had his head placed on London Bridge beside that of William Wallace. John, Earl of Atholl, because of, rather than despite, his relationship to the English king, was hanged on high gallows (30 ft higher that others, according to one source) before being decapitated and burned.

Within three months of his coronation, Robert Bruce was a hunted man, fleeing for safety with a few close supporters. According to a popular English story of the time, Bruce's wife had told him that he was a 'summer king' and that his kingdom would not last until winter. This prediction seemed close to fulfilment in late August–early September as Bruce tried to flee the mainland, escaping westwards via Lennox and Loch Lomond to Bute and then finally to Dunaverty near the Mull of Kintyre. He stayed there a few days in September 1306 before fleeing by boat to the island of Rathlin, 13 miles across the sea, just off the coast of Antrim.

Robert Bruce disappeared from record for the next four-and-a-half months in the winter of 1306–7. John of Fordun details Bruce's sufferings after his coronation but gives few clues as to his whereabouts during this time:

The main door, Lanercost Priory, founded by Robert de Vaux, c. 1166. The priory was situated just a few hundred yards south of Hadrian's Wall and was therefore very vulnerable to Scottish raiding parties after 1296.

> His mishaps, flights and dangers; hardships, and weariness; hunger, and thirst; watchings and fastings; nakedness, and cold; snares, and banishment; the seizing, imprisoning, slaughter, and downfall of his near ones, and – even more – dear ones (for all this he had to undergo, when overcome and routed in the beginning of the war) . . .
>
> Now passing a whole fortnight without food of any kind to live upon, but raw herbs and water; now walking barefoot, when his shoes become old and worn out; now left alone in the islands; now alone fleeing before his enemies; now slighted by his servants; he abode in bitter loneliness. An outcast among the nobles, he was forsaken; and the English bade him be sought for through the churches like a lost or stolen thing. And thus he became a byword and a laughing-stock for all, both far and near, to hiss at.

Two northern English chronicles, the *Lanercost Chronicle* and *Guisborough Chronicle*, thought that Bruce was lurking either in the 'remote isles of Scotland' (*Lanercost*) or 'the furthermost isles of that country' (*Guisborough*). Edward I thought that Bruce was hiding in the isles

Kildrummy Castle. This site was, briefly, sanctuary for Robert Bruce's wife and daughter in 1306. Its commander, Neil Bruce, Robert's brother, was captured and beheaded after an English siege.

between Scotland and Ireland. Bruce's later biographer, John Barbour, felt that he remained hidden away on Rathlin Island. Other possibilities in this mystery are Ireland, Norway and/or the Orkneys and Shetland.

The suggestion that Norway and/or the Orkneys and Shetlands were possible refuges is probably based on the fact that Bruce's wife and daughter were heading in the direction of Orkney after escaping from Kildrummy Castle just before Aymer de Valence captured it. Bruce's sister, Isabel, had married into the Norwegian royal family and by this time was the widow of the late King Eric and sister-in-law to King Hacon. Isabel was an influential lady and could help provide refuge for her brother either in the Orkneys or in Norway itself. There are reasons too why Ireland can be put forward as the major hiding place of Robert Bruce. The Bruce family from their main base in south-west Scotland had naturally developed links with Ireland as had their allies, the Stewarts. The Turnberry Band of 1286 had involved both Bruces and Stewarts in an agreement to support the Earl of Ulster and Thomas de Clare. The Earls of Carrick had long interfered in the affairs of Ireland and the Bruce Earls of Carrick seem to have maintained the tradition. The Earls of Carrick

Lanercost Priory. An Augustinian priory founded in 1166, Lanercost gives us, through its chronicler, one of the best narratives of the Scottish wars; it suffered much from Scottish raids. In 1306 Edward I, near to death, stayed at Lanercost Priory for six months before moving to Burgh on Sands where he died.

Clattingshaw Loch. Near Glen Trool, this loch is part of a wild landscape suitable for a Bruce ambush.

owned land on the Antrim coast and it seems Robert Bruce could well have used this strategic link when he needed a refuge.

Allies of Bruce who were known to be actively supporting him perhaps give the best clues to Bruce's whereabouts in the winter of 1306–7. Like the Bruce Earls of Carrick, James Stewart also had land and a castle in Ireland on Lough Foyle. The mention of an Irish 'kinglet' in support of Bruce's two brothers, Thomas and Alexander, when they relaunched Bruce's military campaign in Galloway early in 1307 also suggests that Bruce was present in Ireland while he was a fugitive. The *Guisborough Chronicle* also refers to many Irishmen in his following on Bruce's return from the isles to Kintyre. The Macdonalds of Islay, too, are known to have given crucial support to Bruce at this time, which suggests the Hebrides may have featured during Bruce's exile. John of Fordun also refers specifically to Christian (or Christine) of the Isles using her power and influence. Christian was the daughter and sole heir of Alan Macruarie, Lord of Garmoran, and, therefore, had control over many areas in the west suitable for a fugitive: Knoydart, Rum, Moidart, Eigg, Uist and Barra among others. Christian was also related to Bruce through marriage to Duncan of Mar, a brother of Robert Bruce's first wife.

John of Fordun reports that Robert Bruce 'after endless toils, smart, and distress, got back, by a round-about way, to the earldom of Carrick'. It seems that Bruce moved from place to place – very wise for a fugitive – but that the landing at Carrick and those with whom he is known to have formed alliances would suggest he spent time at Rathlin, Ireland and the southern Hebrides rather that further north in the Orkneys or Norway.

It is, of course, during the trials and tribulations of this obscure time in Bruce's career that the famous legend of Robert Bruce, the 'Cave and the Spider', belongs. The legend's first appearance was once thought to have been in Scott's *Tales of a Grandfather*. It has been discovered, however, that it actually appeared 200 years earlier in a history of the Douglas family by Hume of Godscroft. According to the story here, it was James Douglas, Bruce's close friend and ally, who saw the spider. According to the book, Douglas told the tale to Bruce while he was a fugitive in the Hebrides and consulting with his companions about plans for his and their futures. In the story Douglas likens Bruce's losses in battle by the winter of 1306–7 to the efforts of a spider climbing a tree with his web and failing twelve times. The spider climbed the tree on his thirteenth attempt and Douglas encouraged Bruce to follow the spider's example and try his fortune again.

Robert Bruce certainly returned to the mainland in early 1307 to continue his campaign; however, his renewed efforts began ignominiously. He split his forces in two and, while he returned to Carrick, landing near the earldom's chief castle at Turnberry, his two brothers, Alexander and Thomas, landed in Galloway where they were opposed by the Macdowells. Bruce's brothers were captured and their forces defeated.

They suffered the same fate as Neil Bruce: they were taken from Galloway to Carlisle, together with Reginald Crawford, and then hanged and beheaded. This was a particularly heavy blow to the Bruce family who had suffered so much in 1306.

As for Robert Bruce himself, it was natural for him to return to Carrick and to Turnberry, not only to muster support but also to gather money for future campaigns. He had already sent agents to Carrick late in 1306 to arrange the collection of his Martinmas rents in Carrick. The task facing him in 1307 was a daunting one. He may have hoped, when he returned, that Edward I had died as he was gravely ill at Lanercost Priory and had remained there for some time. In fact, Edward I was still alive and Bruce himself had very few men and was surrounded by strategic castles, such as Turnberry and Ayr, controlled by the English and their Scottish allies. Only certain strategies could possibly work in these circumstances. Tactics to be used would include surprise attacks and quick retreats, the burning of enemy lands, the slighting of castles so that they could be of no value to an enemy, and the winning of support through fear.

Given the precarious nature of Bruce's position in 1307, it is somewhat surprising to read suddenly, in Scottish sources, of two significant victories for Robert Bruce at Glen Trool (in April) and Loudoun Hill (in June). Much has been made of these two victories, especially by Bruce's biographer, John

Overleaf:
Glen Trool, the setting for Robert Bruce's military comeback (1307) as a guerrilla leader in suitably wild terrain.

Robert Bruce's monument, Glen Trool. Although the military achievement of Bruce at this battle has been exaggerated, the skirmish helped to establish his credentials as resistance leader.

Barbour, as the turning points in Bruce's fortunes. Recent assessment of Glen Trool (C. McNamee, *The Wars of the Bruces* [1997]) suggests it was less of a Bruce triumph and rather a failed attempt to ambush the Treasurer of England. Glen Trool was certainly in wild country, very suitable for ambush, but English sources do not speak of a Bruce victory, only of the 'chase against Bruce between Glentrool and Glenheur'. According to them, Bruce was still a hunted fugitive and certainly not a victor in battle. The skirmish at Loudoun Hill (on about 10 May) appears to have resulted in a slightly more positive outcome for Bruce. Loudoun Hill (a few miles east of Kilmarnock) was, like Glen Trool, in ideal terrain to mount an ambush that would discomfit a cavalry force. Aymer de Valence's force, it is agreed, was forced to withdraw but, again, Barbour has exaggerated the scale and significance of this 'incident'. Bruce was still pursued as a fugitive. He was mainly hunted from mid-July by John Macdougall of Argyll, a relative and ally of the Comyns, who had been given responsibility for the garrison and castle at Ayr. It should not be forgotten that Bruce's conflict at this stage was as much a civil war as a war against the English with the aggrieved Comyn family and their vast network of allies very actively involved with the English against their common enemy, Bruce.

The impact of Glen Trool and Loudoun Hill on the progress of the war was minimal in strategic terms. It does appear, however, in May 1307 that these skirmishes and Bruce's ability to evade capture were having positive effects on morale. According to a letter from the English court at Carlisle in mid-May, 'the king had been enraged because [Valence] the Guardian of Scotland and other folk had retreated before King Hobbe without doing any exploit'. A Scottish lord, writing (from somewhere in Angus) at the English Court, noted Bruce's burgeoning support:

> I hear that Bruce never had the goodwill of his own followers or of the people generally so much with him as now. It appears that God is with him, for he has destroyed the King Edward's power among English and Scots. The people believe, as I have heard from Reginald Cheyne, Duncan of Frendraught and Gilbert of Glencarnie, who keep the peace between the Mounth and on this side, that if Bruce can get away in this direction or towards the parts of Ross he will find the people all ready at his will more entirely than ever, unless King Edward can send more troops for there are many people living loyally in his peace so long as the English are in power. May it please God to prolong King Edward's life, for men say openly that when he is gone the victory will go to Bruce.

Barbour may have overstated the military impact of Glen Trool and Loudoun Hill but there is no doubting from this letter that a movement in support of Bruce was growing and that the Comyns and their associates in Scotland were more in need of English military backing than ever before. Bruce, it seems, was developing a groundswell of popular support in the same way as Andrew de Moray (in the north) and William Wallace (in the south-west) had done in 1297. The letter goes on to say, 'preachers have told the people that they have found a prophecy of Merlin, that after the death of "le Roy Coveytons" the people of Scotland and the Welsh shall band together and have full lordship and live in peace together to the end of the world'. The northern English *Chronicle of Lanercost* supported this message commenting that, despite the cruel repression of Bruce's followers in 1306, 'the number of those willing to strengthen him in his kingship increased daily'.

As early as 13 March 1307, Edward I himself had shown an awareness of Bruce's growing support and the reasons behind it: 'As some persons, he understands, interpret his late ordinance for settling Scotland as too harsh and rigorous, which was not his intention, he commands him to proclaim throughout Scotland that all who have been compelled by the abettors of Robert de Brus to rise against the king in war, or to abet Robert innocently by his sudden coming among them, shall be quit of all manner of punishment.' (Letter of Edward I to Aymer de Valence and his chief officials in Scotland.)

The nature of Bruce's following is interesting. There were those, like him, who were aggrieved, dispossessed landowners. An example of this was James Douglas, determined to recover the heritage that had been granted to Robert Clifford by Edward I, and willing to join Bruce as long as that was in his own interests. Others like him were Gilbert Hay and William Gourlay. The correspondence from the English Court also suggests a reaction to the 'harshness' of English administration and this may explain the 'popular' support building up even in areas like Ross where aristocratic leaders were pro-Comyn. Bruce's cause was also helped by the speed of movement of his forces in assaults, ambushes and surprise attacks. In the early years of Bruce's campaign there are certainly examples of his use of fear to win support. He was quite prepared to employ a terror campaign against his enemies in Galloway, for instance. Bruce's brother Edward and Lieutenant James Douglas '. . . invaded the people of Galloway, disregarding the tribute [ransom] which they took from them and in one day slew many of the gentry of Galloway' (*Chronicle of Lanercost*). Bruce could be quite unscrupulous in persuading key individuals to support his cause. Bruce forced a reluctant Malise, Earl of Strathearn, for example, to do homage after his associates had kidnapped him and threatened him with hanging. Fear of Bruce was clearly an incentive for some to pledge their allegiance to the new Scottish king but generally the motivation for supporting Bruce was mixed. Correspondence from the English Court or from Edward's officials in Scotland in 1306 and 1307 suggests that English reinforcement and an English royal presence were necessary to bolster the position of the Comyns and their associates in Scotland. Edward I's death at Burgh-on-Sands on 7 July 1307 was a major blow for the Comyns as well as for English interests in Scotland.

KINGSHIP AND THE
CAMPAIGN FOR
POWER

The kingship of Robert Bruce undoubtedly received a huge boost in morale from both Edward I's death and the inertia of Edward II in his early years as king. Edward I had made plans for a further Scottish campaign prior to his death. His son, Edward II, started as if he would carry out his father's campaign but on 25 August he abandoned it, and was not to become personally involved in the Scottish campaign for a further three years. English chroniclers draw sharp contrasts between Edward I and Edward II as military leaders. There is no doubt to the chronicler of Lanercost that the internal political disputes in England gave Robert Bruce much greater freedom of movement in Scotland and probably encouraged men to support him more readily: 'While all these affairs were being transacted, Robert Bruce, with his brother Edward and many of his adherents, was moving through Scotland wherever he liked, in despite of the English guardians, and chiefly in Galloway, from which district he took tribute under agreement that it should be left in peace; for they were unable to resist him because of the large number of the people who then adhered to him.' The replacement of a strong Edward I by a weak Edward II was exacerbated when Aymer de Valence's role as lieutenant of Scotland during the crises caused by Bruce's usurpation came to an end. He was replaced by the ineffective John of Brittany in October 1307. Bruce was now relatively free because of inept English leadership to tackle his chief enemies in Scotland, the Comyns of Badenoch and Lochaber as well as the Comyns of Buchan, the Macdougalls of Argyll and the Earl of Ross. He took advantage of the respite from active English military intervention in Scotland to lead his army northwards at the end of September 1307. Control over northern Scotland was a necessity before any king (Scottish or English) could effectively realise his power in Scotland as a whole. Robert Bruce's route for his northern campaign has been reconstructed largely from a letter (unfortunately barely readable in places) written by Duncan of Frendraught, Sheriff of Banff, to Edward II in April 1308.

Supplementary information is contained in a letter (October/November 1307) from the Earl of Ross to Edward II.

Bruce sought out as a major first target the Comyn of Badenoch (and Lochaber) castle of Inverlochy in Lochaber. This was one of the strongest castles of the murdered John Comyn as well as one of the most strategically placed, guarding the Great Glen. Archaeological evidence seems to confirm a castle-strengthening programme by the Comyns here as elsewhere between 1260 and 1280. In Scotland, Inverlochy is a rare example of the quadrangular castle (90 ft by 101 ft) with high curtain walls fortified with round towers. It is similar in type to, although not as advanced as, more well known castles in Wales, e.g. Harlech (1283), Flint (1277) and Kidwelly (1275). Towers project from each corner at Inverlochy with one tower, the donjon (Comyn's Tower) being larger than the others. This was apparently planned as a keep with residential accommodation. Beyond the curtain wall is a wide ditch and outer bank. The ditch is closely defined round three sides, the fourth side confronting the River Lochy, which fed the ditch. Although the castle at Inverlochy appeared to provide defence in depth, it was taken by Bruce and his men sometime in October or November 1307. It was captured, not by force, but by 'the deceit and treason of the men of the castle'. Bruce attacked both by the land route across the mountains and by sea up Loch Linnhe. The outcome may have been aided by the truce agreed between Bruce and the Comyns' main allies in that region, the Macdougalls. Bruce, on his way north with his army, made this truce with John Macdougall of Lorn.

From Inverlochy, Bruce's army continued up the Great Glen to Urquhart and Inverness Castles, which was surrendered 'through lack of water and because the earl of Ross would not include him [Gilbert Glencarnie senior, Sheriff of Inverness] in his truce'. Just as the Macdougalls had been frightened into a truce, so it seems had William, Earl of Ross, another important ally of the Comyns in the north. The Earl of Ross's fear is clear from his letter to Edward II in November 1307:

> Be it known that we heard of the coming of Sir Robert Bruce towards the parts of Ross with a great power, so that we had no power against him, but nevertheless we caused our men to be called out and we were stationed for a fortnight with three thousand men, at our own expense, on the borders of our earldom, and in two other earldoms Sutherland and Caithness; and he [Bruce] would have destroyed them utterly if we had not made a truce with him, at the entreaty of good men, both clergy and others, until Whitsun next [2 June]. May help come from you, our lord, if it please you, for in you, Sir, is all our hope and trust. And know, dear lord, that we would on no account have made a truce with him if the warden of Moray had not been absent from the country, and the men of his province would not answer to us without his orders, for the purpose of attacking our enemies, so that we have no help save from our own men.

The warden of Moray was Reginald Cheyne, Lord of Duffus, who was from a family with long associations with the Comyns in the north.

Buchaile Etive Mor. Bruce's bold and rapid march across the mountains in 1307 contributed greatly to his success at Inverlochy and further north.

Black Mount and Rannoch Moor. Robert Bruce would probably have passed this way on his journey north to Inverlochy Castle in 1307.

There clearly was a lot of unease among the aristocratic leaders in the north and a complete lack of co-ordination in facing up to Bruce's forces.

Inverness Castle was 'altogether destroyed to the foundations', a common tactic adopted by Bruce. His force did not have specialist siege weaponry and this policy, therefore, ensured that castles could not be retaken and used against Bruce's forces in the future. Another important castle in the area, Urquhart, was also destroyed. According to the letter of Duncan of Frendraught to Edward II, Urquhart was 'lost for want of keeping'. Alexander Comyn of Buchan, brother of John, Earl of Buchan, had in 1304 held Urquhart Castle, which was regarded as one of the strongest castles in the north in the early fourteenth century, being strategically sited on Loch Ness. It commanded a naturally impressive position on a promontory looking over Loch Ness from its steep north-western shore. Again, however, factors other than purely defensive ones led to its capture. Bruce then moved east to the castle of Nairn, which was also destroyed. Further east the castle at Elgin was besieged and forced to negotiate a truce. The momentum was temporarily broken at Banff when Robert Bruce, not for the last time on his campaigns, fell sick. Duncan of Frendraught describes in his letter how Bruce spent two nights at one of Duncan's manors, Concarn, which he burned with all its grain stores.

Inverlochy Castle. This castle was the chief castle of the Comyns in Lochaber and commanded the entrance to the Great Glen. Crown Copyright: *Royal Commission on the Ancient and Historical Monuments of Scotland.*

Glencoe. Bruce's army's march across mountainous terrain in 1307 was matched by supporting galleys up Loch Linnhe.

Bruce's progress was also halted by the forces of John Comyn, Earl of Buchan, John Mowbray and David of Strathbogie, Earl of Atholl, who had all come to Duncan of Frendraught's assistance. At last it seemed that Bruce's opponents had managed to combine to halt Bruce's successful campaign. Bruce took his force to Slioch near Huntly, where he took up a defensive position in a wooded marsh. The lack of decisive leadership among Bruce's opponents was apparent. For some obscure reason they were 'unwilling to fight with him' on Christmas Day and when they returned for battle on 31 December they found Bruce's army too strong to be attacked. Fordun refers to the Earl of Buchan's force as 'overwhelmed with shame and confusion'. Bruce had retained his army intact and also received some respite as he is reported as being seriously ill at this time, only able to be moved on a litter. Bruce organised a truce with John Mowbray, one of the main leaders of the pro-Comyn/English side, at the beginning of Lent (3 March 1308). Next Bruce moved towards another key Comyn stronghold, Balvenie Castle, an important link between the Comyn lordship of Badenoch and the Comyn earldom of Buchan. Substantial remains at Balvenie testify to a castle much strengthened by the Comyns of Buchan after they had acquired it between 1260 and 1280. Balvenie relied for its strength on a notable outer ditch and massive

Overleaf:
Corran Narrows. Bruce moved galleys up Loch Linnhe to support his army's attack on the Comyn castle at Inverlochy.

defensive walls. The flat-bottomed ditch is wide, averaging 40 ft, and 12 ft deep in places, and enclosed the castle on three sides. The earliest plan reveals a large quadrangular court (158 ft by 131 ft) enclosed by high walls over 25 ft in places and 7 ft thick with towers (now gone) at the west and north corners. There was probably another tower at the east end where there is now a large round tower of sixteenth-century origin. According to the letter of Duncan of Frendraught, Bruce 'utterly destroyed that castle with the land . . . which belongs to Sir Reginald Cheyne, flames sweeping right through it'. This important Comyn castle appears, from this source, to have been out of Comyn ownership since the family's submission in 1304. If it was still in the custody of Reginald Cheyne, warden of Moray, it once again gives a poor impression of the effectiveness of his contribution to the Comyn/English war effort.

Bruce went on to attack the Cheyne castle of Duffus before moving further west to Tarradale Castle in the Black Isle. Alexander Comyn had held Tarradale and Urquhart in 1304. The land near the castle was destroyed and, most likely, the castle was slighted. Bruce then moved east again to attack Elgin Castle for a second time. John Mowbray relieved the siege, Bruce's forces retiring as he approached. After the indecisiveness of Slioch at Christmas 1307, at last a confrontation between the forces of Bruce and those of John Comyn, Earl of Buchan, and John Mowbray took place on 22 May 1308. According to John of Fordun:

> In 1308 [Comyn and Mowbray] with a great many Scots and English were assembled at Inverurie. But when King Robert heard of this, though he had not got rid of his serious illness yet, he arose from his litter . . . and ordered his men to arm him and set him on horseback. When this was done, he too, with a cheerful countenance, hastened with his host against the enemy, to the battleground, although by reason of his great weakness, he could not go upright, except with the help of two men to prop him up. When the opposition saw him and his ready for battle, at the mere sight of him they were scared stiff and, put to flight, they were pursued as far as Fyvie, twelve leagues away.

This battle, on the road between Inverurie and Oldmeldrum, was a decisive one and Bruce's biographer John Barbour, in *The Bruce*, gives a graphic description of the consequent destruction, the herschip (or harrying) of the main Comyn base in the north: 'Now let us go to the king again, who was well pleased at his victory, and had his men burn all Buchan from end to end, sparing none. He harried them in such a way that a good fifty years afterward people bemoaned the devastation of Buchan. The king then took to his peace the north country which obeyed his lordship humbly, so that north of the Mounth there were none who were not his subjects, one and all. His lordship spread always more and more.' Presumably this destruction of people, livestock and farms also paid particular attention to the visible symbols of Comyn lordship in the earldom of Buchan: the castles at Dundarg, Slains, Cairnbulg, Rattray and

Kingedward, the manor house at Kelly (Haddo House), the legal centre of the earldom at Ellon and the religious centre at Deer Abbey.

Bruce's control of northern Scotland, except for Banff, and for a time Aberdeen, was now complete. John Comyn, Earl of Buchan, and John Mowbray fled south to seek support from the English king. In little over a year, after a very unpromising start, Robert Bruce had chased the Comyns from the area where they had established virtually vice-regal power since their acquisition of the earldom of Buchan in 1212. The reasons for such dramatic success, especially the taking of northern castles, some of which were on good defensive sites with good fortifications, seem difficult to fathom. The Bruce army did not have siege engines. Letters to Edward II during the course of the summer, 1307, and afterwards, emphasise the size of the Bruce army as well as its speed to account for the truces won and its relatively unimpeded progress northwards. The surprise element

Bruce's conquest of Scotland, 1307–14.

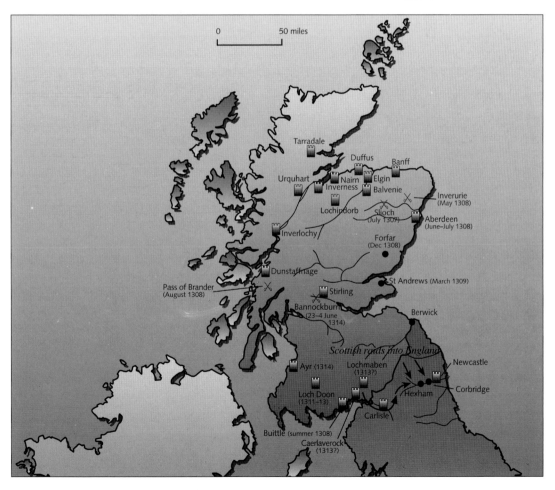

The Great Glen and Loch Lochy. The Comyns exerted control of the Great Glen through the castles of Inverlochy in the south and Urquhart on Loch Ness.

Urquhart Castle. Situated on Strone Point on the western shore of Loch Ness, Urquhart controlled the strategic route along the Great Glen to Inverness.

in Bruce's attacks hardly accords with a very large army. No doubt Bruce acquired some financial resources to pay for mercenaries when Galloway bought off Robert's attacks. He had had support from the north and western isles during his enforced exile from 1306 to early 1307 and he gathered recruits from Lennox, Menteith and from the Macdonalds. He had support in Ross despite the Earl of Ross. However, Bruce's manpower was still, according to Barbour, modest (hundreds rather than thousands) and comprised freeholders and peasants rather that trained troops. The circumstances surrounding the taking of northern castles suggests inadequacies in the castles' defences as much as the strength of Bruce's attack. The joint pro-Comyn and English forces in Scotland acted in a very unco-ordinated manner and seemed to be relying on further English support, which was unlikely to be forthcoming during the winter months. Morale seems, quickly, to have fallen and this would appear to explain examples of treachery and lack of adequate garrisoning and supplies. Quick, guerrilla-type raids from Bruce's forces helped him to pick off his opponents one by one. Success generated its own momentum and increased doubt and indecisiveness among Bruce's opponents, Comyn Earl of Buchan and John Mowbray.

Bruce's campaign in the north was matched by his brother Edward's campaign in Galloway. It was a bloody campaign as reported by the *Lanercost Chronicle*: 'Meanwhile, taking advantage of the dispute between the King of England and the barons, Edward de Brus, brother of the oft-mentioned Robert and Alexander de Lindsey and Robert Boyd and James de Douglas, knights, with their following which they had from the outer isles of Scotland, invaded the people of Galloway, disregarding the tribute which they took from them, and in one day slew many gentry of Galloway, and made nearly all that district subject to them.' Despite John Barbour's claim that Bruce succeeded in taking thirteen castles in Galloway, this overstates Bruce control in the south and south-west, where most of the well-fortified private castles such as Caerlaverock, Dalswinton, Bothwell, Lochmaben, Loch Doon and Dirleton were in English or pro-Comyn hands as well as royal castles such as Wigtown, Lanark, Dumfries and Ayr.

In the north, Robert Bruce continued to strengthen his position. Aberdeen fell in July 1308. Lack of English support contributed to the capitulation of the north to Robert Bruce. Edward II had promised an expedition to Scotland in 1308 and encouraged supporters to take a truce until August when he hoped to lead an expedition into Scotland. However, as contemporary English chroniclers report, the great Court rivalry among the English nobility took priority with Edward II. Edward II also seemed to be waiting for the right moment to strike back in Scotland. The end result was a delayed English response which gave Robert Bruce time to consolidate his support and further weaken the resolve of his Scottish opponents. The only major northern force not under Bruce's military control by mid-August 1308 was that of the Macdougalls. The Macdougalls had made a truce with Bruce as he proceeded north to Inverlochy in 1307. That truce must have ended by August when Bruce was also free from other distractions in the north to concentrate his efforts on Argyll. John Macdougall of Lorn had been ill through the winter of 1307–8 and remained at Dunstaffnage Castle. In March 1308 he wrote a letter to Edward II as full of foreboding as that of William, Earl of Ross, in November 1307. Both complain of the threat from Bruce's large army and the lack of support from their barons, and ask for English aid. John, perhaps, exaggerated his difficulties slightly more:

Robert Bruce approached these parts by land and sea with 10,000 men, they say, or 15,000. I have no more than 800 men, 500 in my own pay whom I keep continually to guard the borders of my territory. The barons of Argyll give me no aid. Yet Bruce asked for a truce, which I granted him for a short space and I have got a similar truce until you send me help. I have heard, my lord, that when Bruce came he was boasting and claiming that I had come to his peace, in order to inflate his own reputation so that others would rise more readily in his support. May God forbid this, I certainly do not wish it, and if you

Balvenie Castle. The castle's strategic position, linking the Comyn lands of Badenoch to the Comyn earldom of Buchan, ensured it was a prime target for Robert Bruce in 1308.

hear this from others you are not to believe it; for I shall always be ready to carry out your orders with all my power, wherever and whenever you wish. I have three castles to keep as well as a loch twenty four miles long [Loch Awe], on which I keep and build galleys with trusty men to each galley. I am not sure of my neighbours in any direction. As soon as you or your army come, then, if my health permits, I shall not be found wanting where lands, ships or anything else is concerned, but will come to your service.

John Macdougall tried to ambush Robert Bruce as Bruce approached Argyll following the line taken by the modern road and railway to Oban. A suitable place for such an ambush was the narrow pass at Brander south of Ben Cruachan (3,689 ft). Barbour, in *The Bruce*, described it as 'so narrow and confined that two men could not ride abreast at some parts of the hillside. The lower side was dangerous, for a sheer crag, high and fearsome, reached down to the sea from the pass. On the other side was a mountain [Ben Cruachan] so rocky, high and steep that it was hard to get by that way.' Macdougall commanded the ambush from a galley on Loch Awe where he was still recovering from his illness. His men hid on the hillside overlooking the track but Bruce out-thought him by sending his own highlanders under James Douglas to climb further up the hillside above Macdougall's men, who were attacked from above as well as below. Macdougall's forces fled to Dunstaffnage hotly pursued by Bruce and his men, who besieged the castle. According to John of Fordun, Alexander Macdougall, John's father,

Duffus Castle, Moray. This castle was regarded as a key northern stronghold and was targeted by Andrew de Moray's 1297 rebellion as well as by Bruce in 1307.

Loch Ness. Robert Bruce marched alongside the west side of Loch Ness to capture and destroy Urquhart Castle.

surrendered the castle after a siege 'of some time'. The strength of the castle would indicate that, if adequately defended, Dunstaffnage could hold out for a long period of time. Barbour, however, reported that Dunstaffnage 'fell in a short time'. Before the castle surrendered, John Macdougall escaped down Loch Awe to his castle of Innis Chonnel from where he fled to England.

With Bruce's latest success in the north, it was hardly surprising that William, Earl of Ross, formally submitted to Bruce near Nairn on 31 October. Bruce seemed to want Ross as an ally in the north and pardoned him after Ross confessed his trespasses. More Scots had come over to his side by 1309, including James Stewart and his nephew, Alexander, Thomas Randolph the younger and John of Menteith. By 1308, Bruce's main opposition, the Comyns and their associates, had been driven out of their main bases in Buchan, Moray and Argyll. Bruce control north of the Mounth was complete but this was certainly not his position further south by 1308. Inroads had been made in the south-west but elsewhere in Scotland Bruce's progress was slow. Rutherglen was taken by Edward Bruce in late 1308 and Bruce's supporters took Forfar in a surprise attack using ladders to scale the walls at Christmas 1308. The inadequacy of the castle garrisoning at Forfar was also evident at Perth, where the commander of the castle, Edmund Hastings, complained that his garrison's pay was twenty weeks in arrears. Edward II's policy from 1307 to 1310 played into Robert Bruce's hands. He abandoned his military campaign in 1307, promised an expedition in 1308 for his allies in Scotland, which was not forthcoming, and in 1309 agreed a general truce until the summer of 1310. He encouraged his garrison commanders at Berwick, Carlisle, Perth, Dundee, Banff and Ayr to take what truces they could. It is clear at Perth and probably at other castles that garrisoning was inadequate. Edward's procrastination in providing resources for the war effort in Scotland allowed Bruce to consolidate his support and gain money as it is known that some truces were paid for.

Edward II's poor resourcing of the Comyn party in Scotland, especially in 1307 and 1308, meant that the Comyns and their associates faced a very demanding task to dislodge Bruce. It would be a mistake, however, to assume that the civil war in Scotland was over in 1308. The opposition to Bruce, the remnants of the Comyn-led government, was still in existence and continued to claim to represent the community of the realm in Scotland in 1309. In Scotland, John Comyn, Earl of Buchan, after being chased from his earldom in 1308, was appointed by Edward II as joint warden of the western marches, i.e. Annandale, Carrick and Galloway, in June 1308. The Macdougalls were encouraged to use their sea power against the Hebrides and Argyll and were placed in charge of a special fleet in 1311. The deaths of three members of the Comyn family between 1306 and 1308 – John Comyn, Earl of Buchan (between 11 August and 3 December in 1308), and his brother Alexander Comyn of Buchan (also in 1308) followed the murder of John Comyn of Badenoch in 1306 – were severe blows to the leadership of the anti-Bruce nobility in Scotland.

From 1308, also, Robert Bruce could begin to use the machinery of Scottish government to strengthen the national and international acceptance of his kingship. Opposition to his position still existed through the remaining members of the Comyn family and their associates. John Balliol was still alive (he died in 1313) and, therefore, Robert Bruce had to justify his position. In his government acts of 1308 and later, Robert Bruce refers to himself, in a very self-conscious way, as the successor to Alexander III, completely ignoring any reference to John Balliol even though as Guardian he had acted in Balliol's name between 1298 and 1300. In 1309 it was still politic either to pretend Balliol's kingship never happened or explain it away as the Declarations of Bruce's first parliament (at St Andrews) did. The St Andrews parliament solemnly upheld Robert Bruce's right to the throne and there were declarations of support from both nobles and clergy. The Declaration of the Clergy was, above all, a propaganda document for Bruce. For the first time, it was declared that Balliol was imposed on the Scots by English force, a belief perpetuated and strengthened by the powerful patriotic narratives of the fourteenth and fifteenth centuries: John of Fordun's *The Chronicle of the Scottish Nation* (1380s), John Barbour's poem *The Bruce* (1375), Walter

Dunstaffnage Castle, Argyll. At the head of Loch Etive, the thirteenth-century Macdougall castle symbolised their power and control of the most important sea-lanes on the western seaboard.

Bower's *Scotichronicon* (1440s) and Andrew Wyntoun's *The Oryginale Cronykil of Scotland* (*c.* 1420). The Declaration of the Clergy represented Balliol as a villain: 'the realm of Scotland was lost by him and reduced to servitude . . . for lack of a captain and a faithful leader'. In contrast, Bruce 'by right of birth and by endowment with other cardinal virtues is fit to rule, and worthy of the name of king and the honour of the realm'.

This propaganda was necessary as the King of France still acknowledged John Balliol as King of Scots in April 1308, though he recognised Robert Bruce as King by July 1309. Also necessary was continuing success in war against the Comyn/English alliance. Success against internal opposition and the English had not been confirmed by 1308. In fact, a rather dour struggle continued until the Battle of Bannockburn of 1314. For his war effort, Bruce needed money. The freeing of important ports, such as Aberdeen, from English control helped to bring in finance from foreign trade particularly with northern Europe. However, one of the most effective methods used by Robert Bruce to gain money (from truces) and supplies was by attacks on northern England. These seem to have started in 1307 and 1308 as cattle raids. Cumberland was affected by 'the thievish incursions of Robert de Brus', as was Northumberland. Raiding intensified in 1311 after Edward II finally mounted a campaign in Scotland from 1310 to 1311. Even this

Dirleton Castle. Standing on a rock in an attractive village, the Vaux's thirteenth-century castle was captured by the English in 1298 and recaptured by Bruce's forces in 1311.

campaign was more of a reaction to Edward's political opposition in England than to the needs of his commanders and allies in Scotland. Yet again Edward II achieved less than he promised. The planned fleet from Ireland to bolster the Macdougall's position in the west was cancelled but the expedition to the east of Scotland did set off, aiming to strengthen the garrisons south of the Forth. Bruce retreated northwards, determined to continue his raid and retreat tactics and avoid confrontation with a larger force. Edward had started his campaign too late to be effective. Contemporary chroniclers thought that Edward II was more interested in discussing peace terms with Robert Bruce than hunting him out of his mountain and woodland retreats. By 1311 Edward II had neither the troops to launch a proper expedition in Scotland (the infantry had already completed their forty-day service by late 1310) nor the financial resources to pay for them.

At the end of July 1311 Edward II left Berwick, the signal for the Scots to step up their raids on northern England and also attempt to capture the major castles in English hands – Edinburgh, Roxburgh, Linlithgow, Dumfries, Stirling, Jedburgh, Berwick and Dundee. Other castles still in English hands included Lochmaben, Loch Doon, Caerlaverock, Dalswinton, Tibbers, Bothwell and Buittle. Money taken from northern England was extremely valuable in maintaining his army in the field against the increasingly isolated English and pro-Comyn forces. As in the period between 1307 and 1310, Robert Bruce was able to take advantage of discord at the English Court to raid northern England more extensively that ever before in 1311. The *Lanercost Chronicle* gives the fullest description: 'Robert, then, taking note that the king and all the nobles of the realm were in such distant parts, and in such discord about the said accursed individual [Piers Gaveston], having collected a large army invaded England by the Solway on [12 August] . . . and burnt all the land of the Lord of Gilsland and the town of Haltwhistle and a great part of Tynedale, and after eight days returned into Scotland taking with him a very large booty in cattle.'

Bruce returned on 8 September marching to Northumberland, passing Harbottle and Holystone and burning the district around Corbridge before moving into the North and South Tyne valleys. The Northumbrians fearing his return arranged a temporary truce and paid him £2,000 'for an exceedingly short time'. In 1312, Piers Gaveston was murdered and there was further political disturbance in England. As a result there was no border defence against Scottish raids and the borders again rendered tribute to Robert Bruce 'in order to have peace for a while'. The Scots, however, burnt Norham 'because the castle did them great injury, and they took away men as prisoners and also cattle'. Robert Bruce gathered an army again about 13 August 1312 and,

> burnt the towns of Hexham and Corbridge and the western parts, and took booty and much spoil and prisoners, nor was there anyone who dared resist. While he halted in

Overleaf:
The Pass of Brander and Loch Awe. Robert Bruce successfully outmanoeuvred an attempted ambush by the Macdougalls at the narrow Pass of Brander. John Macdougall of Lorn looked on from a galley on Loch Awe.

The reverse of the First Great Seal of Robert I. It was in use between 1313 and 1316 and has a number of characteristics following the English pattern. The king is shown on horseback, in chain mail, wearing a globular helmet with a large visor and large crown with three splayed fleurs-de-lis. By permission of the Court of the Lord Lyon.

peace and safety near Corbridge he sent part of his army as far as Durham, which arriving there suddenly on market day, carried off all that was found in the town, and gave a great part of it to the flames, cruelly killing all who opposed them, but scarcely attacking the castle and the abbey. The people of Durham, fearing more mischief from them, and despairing of help from the king, compounded with them, giving two thousand pounds to obtain a truce for that bishopric until [24 June 1313]; which, however, the Scots refused to do unless on condition that they might have free access and retreat through the land of the bishopric whensoever they wished to make a raid into England.

The Northumbrians and the people of Cumberland and Westmoreland gave similar amounts to secure peace. When the truce lapsed in 1313, Bruce again threatened: 'in his usual manner. The people of Northumberland, Westmoreland and Cumberland, and other Borderers apprehending this, and neither having nor hoping for any defence or help from their king (seeing that he was engaged in distant parts of England, seeming not to give them a thought), offered to the said Robert no small sum of money, indeed a very large one for a truce to last [till September 1314].'

Simultaneous with this systematic raiding of northern England, which provided the money, was the targeting of the chief castles of Scotland still in English hands. Bruce gained Perth in January 1313 and Dumfries in February 1313, while his supporters gained Roxburgh in February 1314, Edinburgh in March 1314 and Linlithgow between August 1313 and spring of 1314. Stirling was under siege by Lent in 1314. Bruce's tactics for capturing castles showed that he had no specialist siege weapons. He relied on surprise, night attacks on the walls using rope ladders and the popular support that he had in the countryside. The *Lanercost Chronicle* records the use of the rope ladders in the first attempts to capture Berwick in 1312:

Now these ladders which they placed against the walls were of wonderful construction, as I myself, who write these lines, beheld with my own eyes. For the Scots had made two strong ropes as long as the height of the wall, making a knot at one end of each cord. They had made a wooden board also, about two feet and a half long and half a foot broad, strong enough to carry a man, and in the two extremities of the board they had made two holes, through which the two ropes could be passed; then the cords, having been passed through as far as the knots, they had made two other knots in the ropes one foot and a half higher, and above these knots they placed another log or board, and so on to the end of the ropes. They also made an iron hook, measuring at least one foot along one limb, and this was to lie over the wall, but the other limb, being of the same length, hung downwards towards the ground, having at its end a round hole wherein the point of a lance could be inserted, and two rings on the two sides wherein the said ropes could be knotted. Having fitted them together in this manner, they took a strong spear as long as the height of the wall, placing the point thereof in the iron hole, and two men lifted the ropes and boards with that spear and placed the iron hook (which was not a round one) over the wall. Then they were able to climb up by those wooden steps just as one usually climbs ordinary ladders, and the greater the weight of the climber the more firmly the iron hook clung over the wall.

The attempt on Berwick in 1312 was foiled by a dog's loud barking, but similar methods were successfully employed at Perth in January 1313. Perth was taken by the Scots 'who scaled the walls by night on ladders, and entered the town through the negligence of sentries and guards'. Edinburgh Castle was also taken ingeniously in March 1314. The besiegers attacked the south gate of the castle where strenuous resistance was offered by the besieged but 'meanwhile the other Scots climbed the rocks on the north side, which was very high and fell away steeply from the foot of the wall. There they laid ladders to the wall and climbed up in such numbers that those within could not withstand them, and thus they threw open the gates, admitted their comrades, got possession of the whole castle and killed the English. They razed the said castle to the ground, just as they had done to Roxburgh Castle.' Linlithgow's peel was taken sometime between August 1313 and early 1314 and was, perhaps, the most inventive of Scottish captures. According to Barbour, a husbandman, William Bunnock, concealed eight armed men in his haywain and drove it to the peel, which had been built by Edward I in 1302–3: 'The porter, who saw him clearly coming near the gate, opened it soon, when Bunnock, without hesitation, had the cart move straight on. And when it was set evenly between the checks of the gate, so that no-one could get by, he shouted, "Call all, call all" and then he let the goad drop and quickly cut the traces in two . . .

Corbridge pele tower, Northumberland. This pele tower shows the need for defence in fourteenth-century Corbridge, much visited by Scottish raids because of its importance in the ironware trade.

those who were inside the cart jumped out with agility and soon killed the men of the castle who were near the gate. Then for a while there was shouting; those lying in ambush nearby leapt out, came with drawn swords and took all the castle, without trouble, and slew all of those who were inside.'

There was certainly an increase in the pace of the Scottish war effort in 1313 and 1314. Success in the south-west led to an attack on the Isle of Man by Robert Bruce in May 1313. Rushen Castle was taken in June 1313. Extra Scottish pressure resulted from Bruce's threat in October 1313 to forfeit the lands of all his Scottish enemies if they did not swear fealty to him.

Caerlaverock Castle. A castle impressive in both strength and style, Caerlaverock with its distinctive red sandstone was at the centre of the Anglo-Scottish war in the early fourteenth century.

Auchen/Auchencass Castle, the layout of which shows evidence of English occupation.

This provoked a promise from Edward II in November 1313 to bring an army to Scotland by midsummer 1314. The successful Scottish attacks on Edinburgh and Roxburgh, Edward Bruce's raids into Cumbria and the siege of Stirling were designed to strengthen Robert Bruce's position in Scotland before the English army came.

Walltown Crags. Here Scottish armies swept past Lanercost Priory and Gilsland towards Tynedale.

BRUCE IN TRIUMPH

Perhaps the most remarkable aspect of the Battle of Bannockburn was that such a full-scale confrontation between the armies of Robert Bruce and Edward II ever took place. For his part, Robert Bruce had learned the lesson of Falkirk (1298) and, aware of his force's deficiencies, a lack of knights and a shortage of archers, had engaged primarily in surprise attacks and ambushes. The English chronicler's comment in 1310 that Bruce 'fled in his usual manner' was as true after Bannockburn as before. Edward II, for different reasons, i.e. political squabbles in England and poor financial resources, avoided major confrontation. He soon abandoned the 1307 Scottish campaign organised by his father shortly before his death. Further, he failed to fulfil promises to his supporters in Scotland to mount military campaigns in both 1308 and 1309. When an expedition eventually materialised in 1310, it seemed less to safeguard the interests of his Scottish adherents than to protect Edward's own political interests and the safety of Piers Gaveston from opposition in England. The 1310–11 campaign had a fairly restricted agenda – chiefly to consolidate English garrisons south of the Forth (though his army did, at one stage, reach Perth) – and started too late in the year to have any chance of pursuing and catching Robert Bruce.

As has been seen, Edward II was finally prompted into decisive action by Robert Bruce's threat to his enemies in Scotland, in October 1313, to swear fealty to him as their king or be disinherited. Given Edward II's failure since 1307 to respond adequately with military force to increasingly desperate pleas for assistance from Scottish opponents of Bruce, Edward II was now threatened with the entire collapse of his support in Scotland. He thus announced, on 28 November 1313, that he would arrive with an army in Scotland by 24 June 1314. As far as Robert Bruce was concerned, his piecemeal conquest of Scotland was progressing perfectly satisfactorily on his own terms as key castles of Linlithgow, Roxburgh, Perth and Edinburgh fell into his hands and his support in the country seemed to be growing. It was, by accident, that he was forced into a confrontation with Edward II's army as a result of his brother Edward's arrangement, made with the constable of Stirling Castle, to surrender that castle by 24 June if it was not relieved by Edward's army. Robert Bruce had left the siege of Stirling, which began during Lent 1314, and was undoubtedly angry with his brother's actions

Robert Bruce's statue, Stirling Castle. After Bruce's victory at Bannockburn, he took Stirling Castle and proceeded to dismantle its fortifications.

BANNOCKBURN

The Bruce statue, Bannockburn. Bannockburn secured the reputation of Robert Bruce as defender of the Scottish nation, an image further enhanced by Pilkington Jackson's statue erected in 1964.

The *Chronicle of Lanercost* described the English defeat at Bannockburn as an 'evil, miserable and calamitous day for the English'. Edward II and his Scottish allies lost a great deal, the King being deprived not only of his shield and privy seal but his reputation and credibility. The English monarch even forfeited on the battlefield his court poet, there to record, no doubt, in purple prose the English victory. In return for his release, the poet was compelled to detail the Scottish victory and the reasons behind it:

The commemoration plaque at Bannockburn. The engagement was first known as the Battle of Stirling (by the English) and the Battle of Bannok (by the Scots). The battle was named after a place rather than a stream.

The site of the battle at Bannockburn. Historians have considered four possible sites for the battle; the traditional site marked by the visitor centre and statue is no longer considered the most probable site. (See p. 129.)

While they [the English] spend the night in
  braggartry and revelry with Bacchus
they do wrong to you Scotland, by reviling you
  with empty words
They snooze, they snore: transformed by idle
  dreams
they deem themselves heroes: they overturn the
  bounds of their country
The army unfurls its gleaming banners over the
  field:
but now they are scattered, their manhood is
  unequal to the task.

This indiscipline contrasted vividly with Bruce's inspirational speech to his army on the eve of battle: 'Oh! nobles. My people who value greatly the freedom for which the kings of Scotland have suffered many struggles, dying in the Lord, let all of them now think on the labours we suffered while we have struggled for eight years now, for [our] right to the kingdom, for the honour of freedom.'

The Pilkington Jackson statue of Bruce.

in his absence. Bruce's caution in a situation alien to his fighting instincts is apparent at a number of stages in the ensuing battle.

The English army that moved into Scotland under Edward II consisted probably of 10,000 infantry and over 2,000 cavalry. The force was weakened by the absence of several earls including the earls of Lancaster and Warwick, whose failure to respond to Edward's summons is a reminder of those internal political disputes among the English which so helped Robert Bruce consolidate his position in Scotland after 1307. It was still, however, a much stronger force than Bruce had ever met before. There were leading English nobles such as the earls of Hereford (Humphrey de Bohun), Gloucester (Gilbert de Clare) and Pembroke (Aymer de Valence) and prominent nobles such as Henry Beaumont, Robert Clifford, Hugh Despenser, Marmaduke Tweng and Pain (Pagan) Tiptoft. Prominent in the army, too, were representatives of the Scottish government in exile – John Comyn, son and heir of the murdered John Comyn, his relative Edmund Comyn of Kilbride, the Comyn associate and former Guardian Ingram de Umphraville as well as Robert de Umphraville, Earl of Angus. It should also be remembered that Philip de Mowbray, the commander of Stirling Castle, was from a family closely associated with the Comyn-led Scottish government up to 1304. The position of these Scottish families so opposed to the Bruce 'coup' of 1306 could, perhaps, be seen with hindsight as a hopeless one in 1314. It is certainly true that the absence of effective English support in Scotland

The Bruce statue, Bannockburn. The Pilkington Jackson bronze monument of Robert Bruce was unveiled by HM Queen on 24 June 1964 to celebrate the 650th anniversary of the battle.

since 1307 had reduced their influence in Scotland drastically. However, their hopes to regain their prominent place in Scottish society in 1314 were not ill founded. It is apparent that Bruce had little faith in his ability to defeat full English forces in a pitched battle. Edward II and his more experienced military advisers must have been aware of the Scottish surrender (with little resistance) to Edward I's campaign of 1303–4, which repeated a surprisingly quick Scottish capitulation at the Battle of Dunbar in 1296.

The Scottish army that opposed Edward II in 1314 was almost entirely an infantry force, numbering between 5,000 and 6,000. According to the *Vita Edwardi Secundi* the typical infantryman 'was furnished with light armour, not easily penetrable by a sword. They had axes at their sides and carried spears in their hands. They advanced like a thickset hedge, and such a phalanx could not easily be broken up.' Supporting the infantry there were 500 'light' cavalry. This force met at the Torwood, a stretch of woodland a few miles south of Stirling.

The site of the Battle of Bannockburn has been the subject of much debate by academics and writers with military expertise. The debate itself is thoroughly examined by Professor G.W.S. Barrow (*Robert Bruce*), who concludes that the main conflict, on the second day of the battle, 24 June 1314, was fought on the Dryfield of Balquhiderock. The 'traditional' site marked out by the statue of Robert Bruce and the visitor centre has long since been discredited as the probable site of the battle.

It would be a mistake to conclude that once his army was gathered at the Torwood, Robert Bruce had already decided on a do-or-die battle strategy. He had decided to move his four brigades to the New Park where the woodland gave him the option of a retreat masked by the trees should this be necessary. Philip Mowbray, who came to Edward II to tell him that he was now within 3 leagues of Stirling Castle and had, therefore, in theory, relieved the siege, also reported to Edward the latest intelligence on the Scottish army. He pointed out the difficulties of attacking Bruce with cavalry in the New Park where the Scots had blocked the narrow forest roads ready for ambush. Mowbray also thought the Scottish army, because of its size, would retreat. Bruce had, it seems, selected a favourable defensive site suitable for his predominantly infantry force. This position, according to Barbour, was strengthened further by the digging of pits, camouflaged with twigs, and designed to disturb a cavalry charge. The advance party of the English army, commanded by the earls of Hereford and Gloucester, may have been sent out to ensure that the Scots did not escape overnight as the day (23 June) was already well advanced. The English forces, until the last, thought that the Scots would retreat when approached and when the advanced group spied Scots in the wood they naturally assumed that they were 'straggling . . . as if in flight'. Overconfidence in the English ranks was illustrated in the famous

Dunbar Castle, with its harbour, was a key strategic site in the Anglo-Scottish war.

opening encounter between Henry de Bohun, the Earl of Hereford's nephew, who espied Robert Bruce himself slightly separated from his colleagues. John Barbour (*The Bruce*) reports the encounter:

And when Gloucester and Hereford were coming near with their division there came riding in front of them all, helmet on his head and spear in his hand, Sir Henry de Bohun the brave, who was a valorous and bold knight . . . armed in fine good armour. [He] came on his horse almost a bow-shot in front of all the others who were there, and knew the king, because he saw him arranging his men in line thus, and by the crown also that was set upon his basnet, [so] towards him he went with speed. And when the king saw him coming so openly in front of all his comrades, he set his horse towards him at once. And when Sir Henry saw the king come on without dismay, he rode to him full tilt. He thought that he would beat him quite easily, and have him at his will, because he saw him so poorly horsed. They closed together in a direct course; Sir Henry missed the noble king, and he, standing in his stirrups, with an axe that was both hard and good, struck him a blow with such great force that neither hat nor helmet could stop the heavy clout that he gave him, so that he cleaved the head to his brains. The hand-axe shaft broke in two and [de Bohun] fell flat to the ground, because his strength had gone. This was the first blow of the fight, [and] was mightily done. And when the king's men saw him, right at the first encounter, without hesitation or trepidation, slay a knight thus with one blow, they took such encouragement from it that they advanced right boldly. When the Englishmen saw them advancing stoutly, they were greatly cast down, especially because the king had slain that good knight so quickly, [so] that they all withdrew and no-one dared stay to fight, so [much] did they fear the king's might.

It was the expectation of a Scottish retreat that led Robert Clifford and Henry Beaumont, who had not seen the incident involving Bohun, to 'make a circuit of the wood to prevent the Scots escaping by flight'. The Scots took advantage of the isolation of this group from the main force and according to the *Lanercost Chronicle*: 'The Scots did not interfere until they [the English] were far ahead of the main body, when they showed themselves, and cutting off the king's advanced guard from the middle and rear columns, they charged and killed some of them and put the rest to flight. From that moment began a panic among the English and the Scots grew bolder.' The schiltrom of Moray had stayed firm and disciplined against the English cavalry charge and heavy losses had been inflicted on the English cavalry, some of whom fled to Stirling Castle, while the remainder returned to the main body of the English army. Undoubtedly their return would not have enhanced English morale, which would also have been reduced by their uncomfortable overnight camp 'upon a plain near the water of the Forth beyond Bannockburn [the Carse of Balquiderock] an evil, deep, wet marsh, where the said English army unharnessed and remained all night, having sadly lost confidence and being too much disaffected by the events of the day'. They expected a stealthy night attack from the Scots and so rested little.

Yet even with this success, on 23 June, Bruce hesitated when faced with the thought of confronting the mass of the English army the next day. According to Barbour's *The Bruce*, the Scottish king asked his men whether they should stay and fight or withdraw. Similarly, Thomas Gray in his *Scalacronica* reported:

> The Scots in the wood thought that they had done well enough for the day, and were on the point of decamping in order to march during the night into the Lennox, a stronger country, when Sir Alexander de Seton who was in the service of England and had come thither with the king, secretly left the English army, went to Robert de Brus in the wood, and said to him: 'Sir, this is the time if ever you intend to undertake to re-conquer Scotland. The English have lost heart and are discouraged, and expect nothing but a sudden, open attack.' Then he described their condition, and pledged his head, on pain of being hanged and drawn, that if he [Bruce] would attack them on the morrow he would defeat them easily without [much] loss.

The projected retreat of Bruce's forces to the Lennox was a natural reaction of an experienced guerrilla leader who had triumphed in a skirmish but was happier to fight on terrain more naturally suited to surprise attacks than Bannockburn. Whether influenced by Seton or the confidence of troops, whose morale must have been high after the successful skirmishes of 23 June and following a number of years of military success since 1307, Bruce's army advanced into the open with three divisions of infantry in schiltroms, according to English sources (four divisions according to Barbour's *The Bruce*). The battleground chosen by the Scots was in a confined area, between woods and marsh, and the Scottish infantry appear to have occupied its entire width. This restricted both the English archers and English cavalry, and the former failed to disturb the Scottish schiltroms. The first charge of the English cavalry, led by the Earl of Gloucester, is graphically described in the *Lanercost Chronicle*: 'Of a truth, when both armies engaged each other, and the great horses of the English charged the pikes of the Scots, as it were into a dense forest, there arose a great and terrible crash of spears broken and of destriers wounded to the death, and so they remained without movement for a while.' According to the Lanercost chronicler, 'In the leading division were killed the Earl of Gloucester, Sir John Comyn, Sir Pagan de Typtoft, Sir Edmund de Mauley and many other nobles'. The Earl of Gloucester's death, as described in the *Vita Edwardi Secundi* (author unknown), was probably typical of that of other knights isolated by the failed cavalry charge: 'The earl withstood him [James Douglas and his division] vigorously, penetrated their formation once and again, and would have achieved a triumph if he had had faithful companions. But lo! Suddenly the Scots make a rush, the earl's horse is killed and the earl falls to the ground. He lacked a defender and burdened by the excessive weight of his body [armour] he could not easily get up.'

The failure of the leading division of English cavalry caused tumult and chaos behind them. The detailed report of the *Lanercost Chronicle* reflects the difficulties that the English army were in.

> Now the English in the rear could not reach the Scots because their leading division was in the way, nor could they do anything to help themselves, wherefore there was nothing for it but to take to flight. This account I hear from a trustworthy person who was present as eye-witness . . .
>
> Another calamity which befell the English was that, whereas they had shortly before crossed a great ditch called Bannockburn, into which the tide flows, and now wanted to re-cross it in confusion, many nobles and others fell into it with their horses in the crush, while others escaped with much difficulty, and many were never able to extricate themselves from the ditch; thus Bannockburn was spoken about for many years in English throats.

According to Thomas Gray's *Scalacronica*, 'Those who were appointed to [attend upon] the King's rein, perceiving the disaster, led the King by the rein off the field towards the castle [Stirling]'. This was the signal for a general retreat. The commander of Stirling Castle, Philip de Mowbray,

Brough Castle. The castle, occupying a key position on the Carlisle to York route, was strong enough to resist attack but helpless to deter the Scots from burning Brough town in 1314.

refused the King entry because the castle had not been relieved and he had, by the terms of his agreement with the Scots, to surrender it to Robert I. The castle was surrendered and Mowbray made his peace with the Scottish king. This meant that Edward II and his chief companions, Hugh Despenser and Henry Beaumont, 'with many mounted and on foot, to their perpetual shame fled like miserable wretches to Dunbar Castle . . . At Dunbar the king embarked with some of his chosen followers in an open boat for Berwick, leaving all others to their fate.' Another large contingent including the Earl of Hereford, the Earl of Angus, John de Segrave, Antony de Lucy and Ingram de Umphraville fled towards Carlisle. They were, however, captured at Bothwell Castle where they were initially received in safety by the commander, Walter Gilbertson, who proceeded to change sides, make them all his prisoners and hand them over to the Scots. The *Lanercost Chronicle* added that 'after a lengthy imprisonment [they] were ransomed for much money'.

Bannockburn had many consequences. For Scottish nationalist writers of the fourteenth and fifteenth centuries, it became the ultimate victory

Overleaf:
Swaledale, one of the main routes followed by Scottish armies on their way home to Scotland from raids in Yorkshire.

in a holy war and made Robert Bruce the ultimate hero of the national cause. It is too easy to let those views predominate which are given with the benefit of hindsight. Undoubtedly Bannockburn was a decisive Scottish victory but the war was not over. Edward II still claimed to be the overlord of Scotland and, though fortunate not to be captured at the battle, was not prepared to give up the fight. To contemporaries, Bannockburn had not confirmed the failure of English attempts to conquer Scotland, but it had endorsed the political position of Robert Bruce as King of Scots after the coup of 1306: 'After the aforesaid victory Robert de Brus was commonly called King of Scotland by all men, because he had acquired Scotland by force of arms' (*Chronicle of Lanercost*). It emphasised Robert Bruce's transformation from a usurper king with minority support in Scotland in 1306 to a king whose piecemeal victories over families that had formed the Scottish political establishment in the second half of the thirteenth century earned him the leadership of the Scottish political community his family had sought for such a long time. The main casualties of Bannockburn were the Comyn family. John Comyn of Badenoch, the leader of the Comyn 'party' was killed at Bannockburn together with Edmund Comyn, Lord of Kilbride. The realistic hopes that the Comyns would be returned to political power in Scotland after an English victory over Bruce were shattered. Even though opposition to Bruce's regime in Scotland lingered on and certainly affected Bruce's actions as king, the Bruces rather than the Comyns or Balliols were now seen as the protectors of Scottish independence. To consolidate this position, his government needed money, and in this respect Bannockburn was very successful. The ransom of English noble prisoners, the supplies, arms and clothing captured and the other plunder taken greatly benefited Bruce's finances. The *Vita Edwardi Secundi* claimed, 'our costly belongings were ravished to the value of £200,000'. The capture of two very strong castles in Scotland, Stirling and Bothwell, as well as winning over Philip Mowbray and Ingram de Umphraville to his side, further strengthened Bruce's military and political position. On a personal note, Bruce so badly hit by family losses in 1306 and 1307 was able to exchange the Earl of Hereford for his queen, daughter Marjory and sister Mary.

Robert Bruce's position and political control within Scotland in 1314 had never been so secure. In November 1314, an act was passed in a parliament held at Cambuskenneth Abbey near Stirling to force waverers holding land in Scotland and England to choose between loyalty to Bruce or England. Yet his failure to win recognition of his kingship from Edward II, despite the severe English loss at Bannockburn, ensured that Bruce had to extend his campaign outside Scotland. In particular, vast areas of northern England as far as the Humber were to be affected by Bruce's campaigns from 1314 to the Treaty of Edinburgh (1328) as

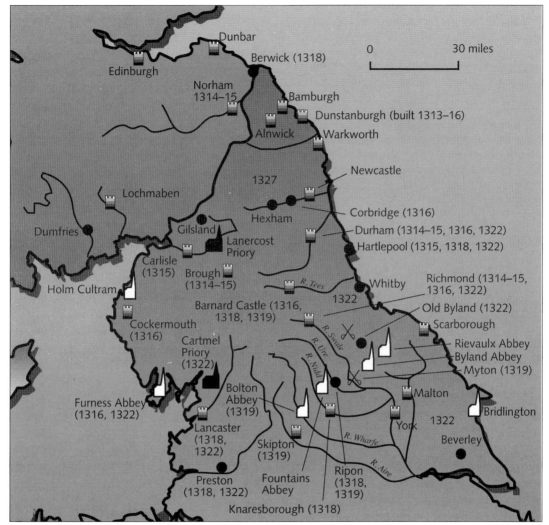

Main areas affected by Scottish raids, 1314–27.

Bruce pressurised Edward II for this recognition. Ireland too would be involved in the new strategy. Berwick and Carlisle, the chief border towns still under English military control, received particular attention. Soon after Bannockburn, Edward Bruce and Thomas Randolph led a Scottish raiding party into England via Norham and down the east coast of northern England, turning at Richmond and returning to Scotland through Swaledale in a north-westerly direction. According to the *Lanercost Chronicle*, which provides good detail of these raids, the Scots 'occupied both North and South Tynedale – to wit Haltwhistle,

The East Window of York Minster. Though threatened by Scottish attack between 1315 and 1322, York prospered in war and peace in the fourteenth century. The East Window (1405–8) is proof of this prosperity.

Hexham, Corbridge and so on towards Newcastle, and Tynedale did homage to the King of Scots and forcibly attacked Gilsland and the other adjacent districts of England'. There was little resistance to their progress except at the Rerecross where a garrison from Carlisle Castle led by Andrew de Harclay was worsted in the skirmish. The Scots were bought off in Durham and Cumberland but they still carried off much plunder, cattle and prisoners. They also burnt the towns of Brough, Appleby, Kirkoswald, Scotby and Penrith. The Augustinian priory at Lanercost, as with other monastic sites in northern England, was seen in this and later raids as an invaluable source of commodities, especially cattle. Monasteries, unlike castles, were seen as easy targets and Scottish raids tended to avoid strong castles such as Berwick, Newcastle, Durham, Richmond and Carlisle. Robert Bruce himself led a raid into Northumberland to regain the lordship of Tynedale.

The purpose of the raids after Bannockburn was to put pressure on Edward II to recognise, formally, Robert Bruce as king of an independent Scotland. Robert Bruce expressed his desire for peace as early as August 1314 but, despite truces to last into 1315, talks broke down on a number of occasions and 1315 began with the threat of ever more far-reaching raids. The fact that Yorkshire now felt threatened is shown by a reported special meeting of Yorkshire magnates in York Minster. However, 1315 saw a much bolder extension to the war with Edward Bruce's expedition to Ireland in May. This had the result of putting even more pressure on Edward II and his resources by extending the war zone. The *Lanercost Chronicle* described how Edward Bruce and Thomas Randolph, 'Landing in Ireland, and receiving some slight aid from the Irish . . . captured from the King of England's dominion much land and many towns and so prevailed as to have lord Edward made king by the Irish [1316]'. The summer of 1315 also saw raids deep into County Durham – many communities in north-eastern England purchased truces – and an attempt to seize the key town of Carlisle. Robert Bruce did not take part in all raids on northern England but did lead his army into the bishopric of Durham. Again, stealth was an important component in this raid. According to the *Guisborough Chronicle*, which records the raid in great detail, Bruce himself remained in Chester-le-Street while, at his command, James Douglas attacked Hartlepool where he 'despoiled the said town and he led back as captives many burgesses and many women'. Hartlepool, it seems, was specially singled out in 1315 as well as

Barnard Castle, the principal English base of the Balliol family, chief rivals to the Bruces as claimants to the Scottish throne in 1290.

subsequent years. It was, of course, important as a port that could be used for naval engagements against the Scots. Hartlepool's resistance to Robert Bruce, however, would particularly rankle with the Scottish king because, as we have seen, Hartlepool was part of the Hartness fief, one of the very first lordships of the Bruce family. This personal affront to Bruce would seem to explain why the people of Hartlepool were not allowed to buy a truce but were forced to take to the sea in ships.

The confidence of the Scots must have been high as the *Chronicle of Lanercost*, after noting that 'affairs were going everywhere in their favour', gives a detailed account of the Scottish attempts to capture Carlisle, beginning on 22 July:

> The King of Scotland, having mustered all his forces, came to Carlisle, invested the city, and besieged it for ten days . . . Now on the fifth day of the siege they set up a machine for casting stones next to the church of Holy Trinity, where their king stationed himself, and they cast great stones continually against the Caldew gate and against the wall, but they did little or no injury to those within, except that they killed one man. But there were seven or eight similar machines within the city besides other engines of war . . . Meanwhile, however, the Scots set up a certain great berefrai like a kind of tower, which was considerably higher than the city walls. On perceiving this, the carpenters of the city erected . . . a wooden tower loftier than the other, but neither that engine nor any other ever did reach the wall, because when it was being drawn on wheels over the wet and swampy ground, having stuck there through its own weight, it could neither be taken any further nor do any harm . . .
>
> Moreover the Scots had made many long ladders, which they brought with them for scaling the wall in different places simultaneously; also a sow [a siege engine constructed to shelter men while they sapped the foundation of walls] for mining the town walls, had they been able; but neither sow nor ladders availed them aught.

The Scots failed also to fill the moat (with bundles of straw) or cross it with wooden bridges. What is more, the tactics successfully employed against Edinburgh Castle, a diversionary attack on one of the gates, failed at Carlisle. The Scots abandoned the siege on the eleventh day, 'whether because they had heard that the English were approaching to relieve the besieged or whether they despaired of success'. The siege at Carlisle highlighted the weaknesses of Robert Bruce's army in attacking a well-garrisoned and defended town – he did not possess either the equipment or skilled personnel for siege warfare. He also still feared full-scale confrontations with large English armies.

The year 1315 had seen the Scottish attacks take a distinctly western focus and the war efforts in Ireland between 1315 and 1318 certainly diverted Scottish resources from attacking north-eastern England more frequently. However, the failed attempt to capture Berwick in January 1316 suggests Robert Bruce also sought large and more strategic targets to enhance his bargaining position. The second failed attempt by Robert Bruce to capture Berwick, in 1316, again highlighted Bruce's main tactic,

Richmond Castle. Standing high above the River Swale, the castle is remarkable for the survival of so much early Norman stonework.

the surprise attack to compensate for his inadequate siege weaponry: 'the King of Scotland came stealthily to Berwick one bright moonlit night with a strong force, and delivered an assault by land and sea in boats, intending to enter the town by stealth on the waterside between Brighouse and the castle, where the wall was not yet built, but they were manfully repulsed by the guards and by those who answered to the alarm'. Berwick would remain in English hands a little longer but it is increasingly clear that for all Berwick's strategic importance, the resourcing of Berwick was inadequate. This caused the warden of Berwick to write bluntly to Edward II, 'your people are dying of hunger . . . you know that no more than £4,000 in money and in every kind of victual has come since I arrived . . . you should attend to this situation . . . think of your town which you hold so dear; because if you lose it, you will lose all the rest of the north' (*Lanercost Chronicle*).

In view of the intensifying pressure on Carlisle and Berwick, in 1315 and 1316, it is possible, perhaps, that the Scottish raid deep into Yorkshire in the summer of 1316 was the beginning of Scottish pressure on York itself. This raid crossed the Tees at Barnard Castle and reached as far as Richmond in Yorkshire. At Richmond 'the nobles of the district, who took refuge in Richmond Castle and defended the same, compounded with them for a large sum of money so that they might not burn that

Overleaf:
Barnard Castle. Scottish raiding parties often entered Yorkshire via Barnard Castle after 1314 but the castle's natural strength and thirteenth-century additions ensured that only the surrounding estates suffered damage.

141

town, nor yet the district more than they had already done' (*Lanercost Chronicle*). The Scots then turned westwards from Richmond through Swaledale 'laying waste everything as far as Furness, and burnt that district whither they had not come before, taking away with them nearly all the goods of that district, with men and women as prisoners. Especially were they delighted with the abundance of iron which they found there, because Scotland is not rich in iron' (*Lanercost Chronicle*). Monasteries of northern England, especially Cistercian monasteries, had the technology as well as the organisation to be at the forefront of mineral exploitation in the north. Iron was vital in warfare and the Scots frequently raided via Corbridge, another important centre for the iron trade in the north.

The 1316 raid came during a slight lull in the Irish war, which took most of the attention of Robert Bruce and his brother Edward between 1315 and 1318. The Bruces' involvement in Ireland could be seen primarily as the personal mission of Edward Bruce to become king there. He had made his first main target, in 1315, the important town and castle of Carrickfergus. He soon took over the town but did not capture the castle until 1316, by which time he had taken Dundalk. Robert Bruce's personal involvement in Ireland with a large army in 1316 and 1317 would indicate that Ireland was another front, an important one in the struggle with England. Ireland was an important supply depot for England and English campaigns in Scotland, and Carrickfergus was particularly vital for sea traffic between Ireland and Scotland. In 1317 Robert Bruce's presence with reinforcements enabled the Bruces' control to be extended beyond Ulster and into Meath. They arrived at Castleknock and brought panic to the citizens of Dublin, who blamed the Earl of Ulster for not defending them adequately. The Bruces progressed, plundering as they went, through Kildare, Kilkenny and Tipperary. When they reached Castleconnel, they discovered that Donough O'Brien who had invited them there had been ousted by his rival. Hopes of a Gaelic revolt in Munster, and also in Connacht, were dashed. At the same time Edward II appointed Roger Mortimer as his lieutenant in Ireland and provided him with sufficient resources to bring about the defeat of the Bruces. At this point, Robert Bruce returned to Ulster and then home to Scotland. Edward Bruce was defeated and killed at Fochart just north of Dundalk in 1318.

Robert Bruce had others beside Edward II to persuade to recognise his title. Pope John XXII was very reluctant to confirm Bruce's position given the fact that John Balliol had not been formally deposed and Bruce had started his reign as the sacrilegious murderer of his great rival, John Comyn. The need for English goodwill and crusading considerations also contributed to this reluctance. When the Pope sent two cardinals as legates, in September 1317, to impose a two-year truce on the Anglo-Scottish war, they were ambushed at Rushyford, south of

Hill of Slane, Meath, Ireland. The Scots under Robert Bruce travelled from Larne to Slane, which they reached on 16 February 1317. They ravaged the surrounding countryside as they passed through it.

Durham. Scottish involvement cannot be proven but it was in Robert Bruce's interests to prevent the legates reaching Scotland bringing terms unacceptable to his interests as well as the threat of his being excommunicated. Bruce eventually met the legates but took offence when they addressed him as 'Governor of Scotland' rather than king. Bruce's message to the Pope was clear: 'I have possession of the kingdom, my royal title is acknowledged throughout the kingdom, and foreign rulers address me as king. Our father the Pope and our mother the church of Rome seem to be showing partiality among their own children.' Bruce ignored the Pope's two-year truce, which was to run from 1317 to 1319. Within this period he (through the actions of James Douglas and Walter the Stewart), at last, captured Berwick in the first few days of April 1318: 'the Scots treacherously took the town of Berwick through means of a certain Englishman, Peter of Spalding, who being bribed by a great sum of money received from them and by the promise of land, allowed them to scale the wall and enter by that part of the wall where he himself was stationed as guard and sentry. After they had entered and gained full possession of the town, they expelled all the English, almost naked and

THE BRUCES IN IRELAND

Rock of Cashel, Ireland.

Carrigogunnel (Castleconnel) Castle, Co. Limerick. Bruce's 1317 mission in Ireland aimed at joining up with Donough O'Brien, owner of Carrigogunnel. The castle is strongly sited on the southern shore of the Shannon Estuary.

There has been much debate among historians as to why the Bruces opened up another war front in Ireland in 1315. The Bruces themselves appear to have viewed it as an attempt at Celtic solidarity in the face of a common enemy, the English. In his letter to the Kings of Ireland, Robert Bruce wrote: '. . . we and you and our people and your people, free from ancient times, share the same national ancestry and are urged to come together more eagerly and joyfully in friendship by a common language

Rock of Cashel, Ireland. The Scottish force was at Cashel on 18 and 19 March 1317, before turning north to Nenagh and destroying the lands of Edmund Butler, the Justiciar.

and a common custom'. The content may have been more a diplomatic ploy than a clear statement of policy. English chroniclers thought that the Scots were bent on conquest buoyed by their devastation of the English marches and the receipt of large sums of money. In 1317, Robert Bruce sailed to Ireland with a great force 'to conquer that country, or a large part thereof for his brother Edward. He freely traversed all that part of it which was within the King of England's dominion, but he did not take walled towns or castles' (*Lanercost Chronicle*). This hints at the real reason for Bruce's actions. Robert's brother Edward, noted for his arrogance, wanted a kingdom to rule. Robert Bruce sought to support him for his own personal reasons – a friendly Ireland was of benefit to Scottish interests – but it meant he had to sacrifice many resources from his English campaigns until Edward's death in 1318 to provide this backing.

Trim Castle, Co. Meath. This is Ireland's largest and finest castle and noted for its great rectangular tower. Trim was the head of the lordship of Meath and, therefore, important on Bruce's itinerary.

despoiled of all their property . . . Howbeit the castle of the town of Berwick defended itself manfully against the town, but at length [18 June] capitulated through want of victual' (*Lanercost Chronicle*). Soon after the fall of Berwick town, the castles of Wark-on-Tweed, Harbottle and Mitford fell to the Scots. The capture of Berwick and Bruce's return from Ireland marked a new stage in Scottish raiding on northern England.

In May 1318 the Scottish army, according to the *Lanercost Chronicle*, invaded England 'further than usual'. This raid, led by Douglas and Randolph, Earl of Moray – Bruce himself was still preoccupied with Ireland – featured a two-pronged attack into Yorkshire. One Scottish party crossed the Tees via Barnard Castle, the second attacked Hartlepool again before crossing into Yorkshire by way of Yarm. The raid on Hartlepool, a reprisal attack after the townsfolk captured a Scottish ship, renewed the personal animosity between Bruce and the Bruce family's former possession. Chronicle accounts establish the principal routes of the Scottish raids in Yorkshire but a valuable supplementary source is the 'Nova Taxatio' of 1318 – this source, by giving the latest parish valuations, helps to assess those areas most affected by the Scottish raiding parties. In 1318 one Scottish group coming from Barnard Castle probably took ransom at Richmond (as they had done in 1316) before moving on to Ripon 'which town they despoiled of all the goods they could find, and from those who entered the mother church and defended it against the Scottish army they exacted one thousand marks instead of burning the town itself'. Six hostages were taken to ensure payment but two years later the townsfolk still had not paid three-quarters of the amount owed. The exasperated hostages' wives at last, in 1324, petitioned the king to put pressure on the Archbishop of York, who had responsibility for Ripon, to compel the townspeople to pay up. The nearby Cistercian Abbey of Fountains, one of the wealthiest abbeys in northern England, also paid a tribute but it did not escape loss. The Scottish army, apparently, stayed for a while at Fountains Abbey and had destroyed granges and outbuildings 'so badly' according to William Melton, Archbishop of York, 'that all the goods looked after at the said monastery were not enough to sustain the monks of that same monastery'.

The two Scottish armies converged at Knaresborough, the second raiding party having moved through Northallertonshire burning Northallerton before moving on to Ripon and Boroughbridge, which was also burned. At Knaresborough, extensive damage was done with 140 out of 160 houses being destroyed. Encamped in the forest of Knaresborough, the Scots raided Tadcaster and Wetherby before returning to Scotland by their usual westward route. They took with them the cattle that the people of the Knaresborough district had tried to hide in the woods. That cattle formed an important part of Scottish raiding was made evident after they plundered and burnt the town of Skipton-in-Craven 'driving off a countless quantity of cattle. They made men and women captives, making the poor folks drive the cattle, carrying them off to Scotland without any opposition'. Just as Fountains Abbey's granges had been despoiled, so the granges of Bolton Priory were damaged as the Scots approached Skipton. Though the priory itself was not attacked, the prior clearly feared for his life because he fled into Blackburnshire. The Scots returned home up the River Wharfe, Ribblesdale and Lonsdale. Lancaster was another town affected by the Scottish raids.

The year 1319 was noteworthy for an agreement between warring factions in England, principally Edward II and the Earl of Lancaster. Peace broke out between them long enough for their forces to besiege Berwick between 7 and 17 September. The Scots had seemed secure since the capture of Berwick in 1318. They had attacked Dunstanburgh Castle on the Northumberland coast earlier in the year to try to prevent this castle, still under construction, from becoming a launching pad for English attacks. The movement of the English force north coincided with a Scottish army entering Yorkshire by 3 September under James Douglas and Thomas Randolph, Earl of Moray. A number of motives have been put forward to explain the Scottish raid of 1319. According

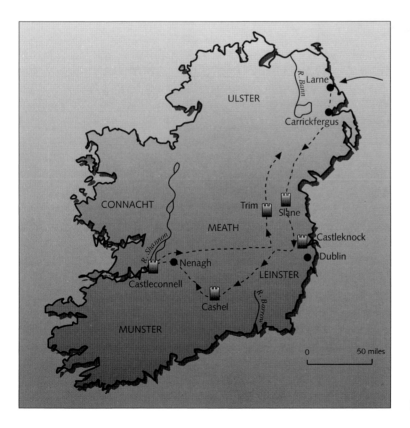

Robert Bruce in Ireland, 1317.

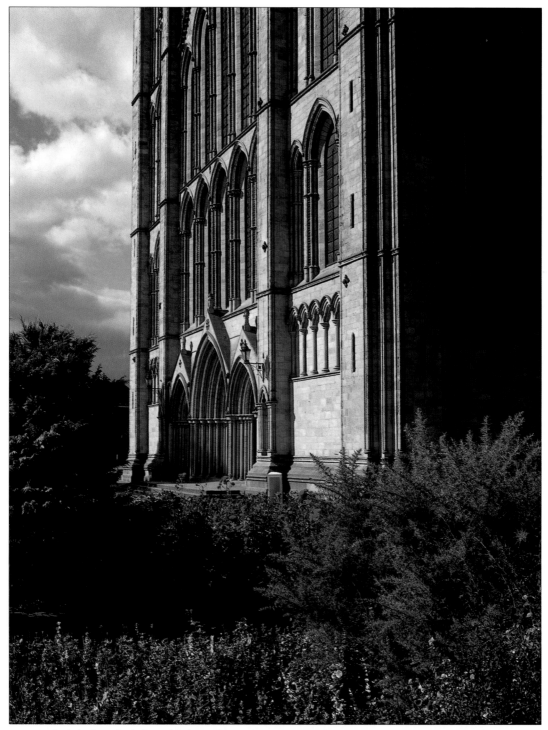

Ripon Cathedral. The cathedral, notable for its thirteenth-century west front, was a valuable bolt-hole for Ripon townspeople when the Scots ravaged the area in 1318 and 1327.

Fountains Abbey, Yorkshire. This magnificent abbey was a base for the Scottish army in 1318. Despite paying a fine, the abbey's rich farmlands were badly hit by Scottish depredations.

to the *Lanercost Chronicle*, the Scots 'not daring to encounter the king of England and the earl of Lancaster, invaded England with an army'. Given the reluctance of Robert Bruce to confront a large English army on other occasions, the raid south could be seen as a diversionary tactic putting pressure on the English to abandon their siege of Berwick. Another source, the *Vita Edwardi Secundi*, suggested more positive reasons for the 1319 invasion of England, that the raid was an attempt 'to carry off the Queen of England, who was staying near York . . . Indeed if the Queen had at that time been captured, I believe that Scotland would have bought peace for herself'. Other sources, too, reflect a fairly common belief that a spy in York had confessed the plot to capture Queen Isabella. If the Queen was staying at Bishopthorpe, in the archbishop's palace near York, the threat to her safety was a real one.

The Scottish attempts to gain important political prisoners become a more significant aspect of their raids after 1318. There was also increasing pressure, after the capture of Berwick, on York itself, the English monarchy's war capital in its fight against the Scots. This has tended to be underestimated in discussion of Bruce's campaigns in northern England. There is evidence

Furness Abbey, Lancashire. A wealthy Cistercian abbey noted for its sheep rearing and iron-ore production, it was often targeted by Scottish raiders for these valuable commodities.

that York itself feared attack after the English defeat at Bannockburn (1314). The Custody of 1315, which reveals the arrangements for the manning of York's walls in time of danger, shows that the city's walls were completed in stone to the height of 12 ft for the central and Micklegate areas, though the Old Baile and Walmgate areas were still defended by wooden palisades. Also complete by 1315 were most of the semi-circular and circular towers jutting beyond the circuit walls – the towers known as the Multangular Tower, St Leonard's or Lendal Tower and Davy Tower were finished by 1315. Anxiety about the security of St Mary's Abbey, where the Chancellor of the Exchequer and Chancery officials were accustomed to stay when the government was in York, is shown in 1318 by the licence granted to the abbey to crenellate its precinct wall, which was also strengthened with towers. The precinct wall between the abbey and the city walls was to remain uncrenellated and restricted in height to prevent the city walls being overlooked by possible enemies.

The fact that the Scottish raiders were very close to York is shown by the need to maintain a garrison at York Castle from 4 to 13 September. The Vicars Choral of York Minster themselves spent 2s on ale and candles so that their section of the city walls could be guarded. The safety of the queen was safeguarded by sending her to Nottingham. The threat to York, and the weakness of the north's defences, in 1319 is highlighted by the instruction given to Archbishop Melton of York to raise a citizen's army to fight the Scots, who were encamped at Myton-on-Swale near Boroughbridge. The Archbishops of York had an honourable historical record as defenders of the north – Archbishop Thurstan led an army to defeat another Scottish invasion, that of David I, at the Battle of the Standard, north of Northallerton in 1138 – but the citizens' army collected by Archbishop Melton in 1319 was a vastly inferior one to that of 1138. The archbishop was not helped by the king's decision a few days earlier to summon the York militia to the Berwick siege. Thus the army led out by the archbishop of York on 12 September was a force 'unskilled in war . . . they marched all scattered through the fields and in no kind of array', comprising citizens, peasantry and a large number of clergy. They faced an experienced Scottish force chosen 'for their fighting ability, fit for every task'. The archbishop's army was badly defeated at Myton-on-Swale, a battle known as the 'Chapter of Myton' because of the large number of clergy in the English force. Among the dead was the Mayor of York, Nicholas Fleming. News of this disaster caused Edward II to abandon the siege of Berwick, which may have been the main objective of Robert Bruce because the Scottish army in Yorkshire, somewhat surprisingly, did not march on York after their victory. Edward II's fear for the loss of York is shown by his grant of a murage (a tax for the strengthening of the city walls) for ten years just a week after the battle. York's wall defences were therefore immediately strengthened.

Overleaf:
Dunstanburgh Castle, Northumberland. Started in 1314/15 by Thomas Earl of Lancaster, it was built as a bolt-hole (from Edward II as well as the Scots) for the earl and the local population.

Instead of attacking York, the Scottish army caused damage and destruction around Boroughbridge but a raiding party did much damage in the forest of Knaresborough and a group even reached as far as Castleford. York was certainly under threat if not attack. The Scots returned home on their normal westerly route through Wharfedale, again doing injury to Bolton Priory's granges before moving into Lancashire. Edward II rather naïvely waited in Northumberland with his army hoping to cut the Scots off as they returned north, but without guarding the westerly route back to Scotland most favoured by previous Scottish raiding parties. The year 1319 ended with a particularly severe raid led by James Douglas and Thomas Randolph in the west reaching as far as Brough in Stainmore, which caused much damage in Cumberland and Westmorland.

If the objective of the 1318 and 1319 raids was to bring pressure on Edward II, it worked in that the English king proposed a truce. The subsequent truce led to peace between November 1319 and January 1322. The break in warfare gave Robert Bruce the opportunity to counter his other enemies. Bruce's relationship with the papacy was at a critical stage. The bull threatening excommunication of the king and interdict on the kingdom, originally issued in May 1318, was renewed. Bruce and four bishops were summoned to the Curia by 1 May 1320 and, when they did not appear, they were excommunicated. It was the Scottish response to this situation that gave rise to the Declaration of Arbroath (1320). This document, which has been described by Professor Geoffrey Barrow in *Robert Bruce* as 'the most eloquent statement of the case for national independence to be produced anywhere in medieval Europe', has done as much as the Battle of Bannockburn to associate the name of Robert Bruce with Scottish independence. The Declaration was a powerful statement of Scotland's independent status and demonstrated an even stronger support for Robert Bruce personally than the Declaration of the Clergy had done in 1309. The authorative language employed gives it a special status as the most treasured document in Scotland's national archives:

But from these countless evils we have been set free, by the help of him who though he afflicts yet heals and restores, by our most valiant prince, king and lord, the lord Robert, who, that his people and his heritage might be delivered out of the hands of his enemies, bore cheerfully toil and fatigue, hunger and danger, like another Maccabeus or Joshua. Divine providence, the succession to his right according to our laws and customs which we shall maintain to the death, and due consent and assent of us all have made him our prince and king. We are bound to him for the maintaining of our freedom both by his right and his merits, as to him by whom salvation has been wrought unto our people, and by him, come what may, we mean to stand. Yet if he should give up what he has begun, seeking to make us or our kingdom subject to the king of England or to the English, we would strive at once to drive him out as our enemy and a subverter of his own right and ours, and we would make some other man who was able to defend us our king; for, as long as a hundred of us remain alive, we will never on any conditions be subjected to the lordship of the English. For we fight not for glory, nor riches, nor honours, but for freedom alone, which no good man gives up except with his life.

This extraordinarily powerful appeal, thought, by some, to be the work of Bernard, Abbot of Arbroath Abbey, was an appeal to the Pope to persuade Edward II to leave the Scots in peace. Though it praises Bruce's role in the nationalist cause, it also recognises that the national cause came before any individual, even Bruce. As the years 1286 to 1306 have shown, Robert Bruce and his family were slow to support the nationalist cause. Military success from 1308 onwards ensured that the nationalist tag stuck to Bruce through history.

The truce years of 1319 to 1321 also showed that Bruce's rule in Scotland, so long opposed within Scotland between 1306 and 1314, was still not without opposition. A conspiracy uncovered in 1320 showed that the old Balliol/Comyn party still existed under the figurehead of William

Bolton Priory. This religious house unfortunately lay on the route frequently taken by Scottish raiders as they turned westward home via Wharfedale. As a result, its estates suffered much damage.

Knaresborough Castle, Yorkshire. On a superb site high above the River Nidd, the few castle remains reflect Edward II's reconstruction after 1307. The town (but not the castle) was severely damaged by the Scots in 1318.

St Mary's Abbey, York. One of the wealthiest monastic houses in Britain, St Mary's Abbey was situated just outside York's city walls. Its precinct wall was started in 1266.

Skipton Castle. Robert de Clifford (killed at Bannockburn) received Skipton Castle in 1310 and started rebuilding. The castle was a refuge from Scottish armies in 1318, 1319 and 1322.

de Soules. Bruce dealt firmly with the conspirators and his leadership remained secure. Edward II's own political position improved suddenly early in 1322 when Andrew Harclay defeated the rebel earls Hereford and Lancaster at the Battle of Boroughbridge. Lancaster was executed and revolt against Edward was over, giving the King far more confidence to invade Scotland again.

Fighting had already restarted early in 1322 shortly after the truce had finished. In the last two weeks of January, Scottish raids under Randolph, Earl of Moray, James Douglas and Walter Stewart targeted the bishopric of Durham, perhaps because a tribute had not been paid. Moray remained at Darlington, while Douglas and Stewart raided Hartlepool (yet again), Cleveland and Richmond. The people of Richmond, as noted by the *Lanercost Chronicle*, 'neither having nor hoping to have any defender now as formerly, bought off the invaders with a great sum of money'. In March, Newcastle felt threatened as the mayor reported an imminent invasion. Although another truce was agreed, preparations for war still continued on both sides. While Edward prepared for an invasion of Scotland, Scottish forces led by Robert Bruce, Moray and Douglas made pre-emptive strikes by way of Carlisle. Bruce's force 'plundered the monastery of Holm Cultram notwithstanding that his father's body was buried there; and thence proceeded to lay waste and plunder Copeland and so on . . . to Furness'. On his way to Furness, Robert burned two water mills of Egremont

Castle. At Furness, he was entertained by the abbot who 'paid ransom for the district of Furness . . . This notwithstanding the Scots set fire to various places and lifted spoil'. They also burned the lands around Cartmel Priory 'taking away cattle and spoil' before moving on to Lancaster where the town, 'except the priory of the Black Monks and the house of the Preaching Friars', was burned. Bruce was now joined by Douglas and Moray who went further south, some beyond Preston in Amounderness, i.e. 80 miles within England. On their way back they stayed outside Carlisle for five days 'trampling and destroying as much of the crops as they could by themselves and their beasts'.

On 1 August Edward II led a large army past Berwick and on to Edinburgh but 'the Scots retired before him in their usual way, nor dared to give him battle'. Robert Bruce's policy of burning land and property and removal of all cattle from the area ensured that Edward II would have difficulty foraging. This problem was seriously exacerbated by the loss of Edward II's supply ships owing to storms and attacks by Flemish privateers. The *Lanercost Chronicle* commented, 'The Scots retired before him in their usual way, nor dared to give him battle. Thus the English were compelled to evacuate Scottish ground before 8 September owing as much to provender as to pestilence in the army; for famine killed as many soldiers as did dysentery.' This illustrates a very successful strategy often implemented by Robert Bruce. Edward II remained in northern England long enough to criticise the commanders of Dunstanburgh, Alnwick, Bamburgh and Warkworth for their inactivity against the Scottish forces who were reasserting themselves in Northumberland. Norham Castle was under siege and, it seems, Wark had already been taken.

Bruce was in a position to launch a large-scale counterattack invading England by the Solway, devastating the area around Carlisle before entering North Yorkshire. Chronicle evidence reflects the importance of this invasion as Bruce 'collected all his forces, both on this side of the Scottish sea and beyond it, and from the Isles and from Bute and Arran'. The *Lanercost Chronicle* gives an interesting insight into Bruce's motives: 'he marched into England to Blackmoor [near Sutton Bank] (whither he had never gone before nor laid waste those parts, because of their difficulty of access) having learned for a certainty from his scouts that the King of England was there'.

Edward II had moved south from Barnard Castle on 2 October, sending out to his northern magnates a summons to meet him on 'Blakehoumor' (Blackmoor). He was, apparently, aware of Bruce on the western march but unaware of the Scottish intelligence about his own exact whereabouts and the threat to his personal safety. He was, however, informed on 12 October, while camped at Rievaulx Abbey, that the Scottish forces were only 15 miles away at Northallerton. They had occupied the Vale of York and destroyed Thirsk and parishes in the area. Ripon paid for a truce.

News of Bruce's army being so close induced desperate orders to Pembroke, Richmond and Beaumont to send their troops to him. The *Lanercost Chronicle*'s suggestion that the main purpose of this Scottish raid was to capture the person of Edward II himself is borne out by the position of Moray's troops at Malton, 15 miles to the south-east of Rievaulx. Given the tactics of Scottish troops in 1318 and 1319, it seems Bruce was determined to capture a hostage of sufficient importance to force recognition of his title and his success since 1308. The Earl of Richmond, John of Brittany, was sent from Rievaulx to 'reconnoitre the army of the Scots from a certain height between Byland Abbey and Rievaulx Abbey, and being suddenly attacked and surprised by them, attempted by making his people hurl stones to repel their assault by a certain narrow and steep pass in the hill'. It seems probable, as Professor Barrow suggests, that the English army of Richmond was positioned on the western edge of Scawton Moor, overlooking Sutton Bank and Roulston Scar. This blocked the way to Rievaulx and as the only alternative route was a 14-mile detour via Helmsley, the Scots launched a direct assault under Douglas and Moray while Bruce commanded his highlanders to climb steep cliffs to attack Richmond from the flank. It was a tactic similar to the one successfully used to overcome the Macdougalls at the pass of Brander. The Earl of Richmond was captured along with Henry de Sully.

Richmond Castle. It served mainly as a refuge for nobles in the area who consistently paid the Scots ransoms to lessen the damage inflicted.

The Declaration of Arbroath (1320). This document became as powerful a symbol for Scottish nationalism as the Stone of Destiny. It certainly enhanced Robert Bruce's 'nationalist' credentials. Ref. SP 13/7. By kind permission of the Keeper of the Records of Scotland.

Edward II, at Rievaulx – 'he being ever chicken-hearted and luckless in war and having [already] fled in fear from them in Scotland, now took to flight in England, leaving behind him in the monastery in his haste his silver plate and much treasure' (*Lanercost Chronicle*) – only just escaped as he had done at Bannockburn. Edward fled via Pickering, Bridlington and Burstwick, from where he went by ship to York. According to the *Meaux Chronicle* the 'Scots entered the aforesaid monasteries of Rievaulx and Byland with violence, put on the clothes of the religious without reverence and all the goods of the monastery, vestments for divine service, consecrated chalices, books and all the sacred ornaments of the altar they carried away with them'. The Scots came to Malton, destroying the castle there before moving on to Beverley, apparently with the captive Earl of Richmond with them. At 'Hunsley [near Beverley] they erected their standard and invaded the rest of the county even to the east sea and towards York on the west,

Warkworth Castle, Northumberland. With the River Coquet providing it with a natural moat, Warkworth was left alone by the Scots apart from a brief siege in 1327.

Rievaulx Abbey. The large monastic precinct (70 acres) here provided an ideal base for Edward II in 1322, although he was nearly captured there by the Scots.

bearing no deference to churches and monasteries; but they destroyed all their substance, they consumed many towns with fire'. Some towns bought peace – Beverley was held to ransom to escape burning. Moray, at Malton, made an agreement with the men of the Vale of Pickering not to burn the area for a ransom of 300 marks; the canons of Bridlington Priory tried to reach an agreement with the Scots to avoid their property being burned. When the Scots reached Bridlington they were offered accommodation in the priory. Tax valuations showing reduced values imply that Robert Bruce was in the Hovingham, Terrington, Sheriff Hutton and Forest of Galtres areas and met up with Moray's force north of York before returning to Scotland prior to 22 October. The reduction of the York garrison at this time implies that the crisis was over but again pressure on both the English king and York itself had been intense. The *Lanercost Chronicle* recorded that the Scottish army had been present in England for one month and three days, the longest period of time that a Scottish army had spent in England, which reflected the build-up of pressure on the English king.

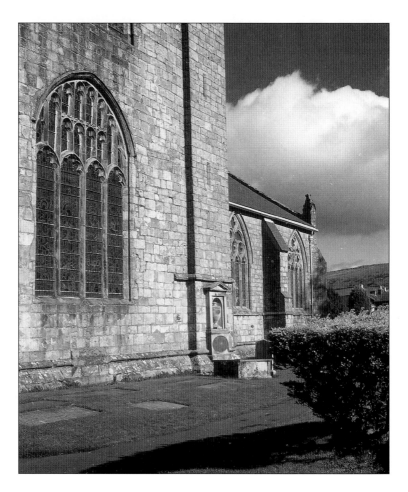

Cartmel Priory. The Augustinian canons of Cartmel Priory had lands burned and cattle seized as Scottish raids intensified in 1322.

Roulston Scar, North Yorkshire. Here the English army attempted, without success, to ambush the Scottish army approaching from the Thirsk area to Rievaulx Abbey and Edward II.

The pressure, however, did not give Robert Bruce the concession he required. It did have an impact on Andrew Harclay, perhaps the leading military commander in England who had been made Earl of Carlisle following his defeat of Lancaster at the Battle of Boroughbridge. Harclay had not been able to respond immediately to Edward's summons at Blackmoor but when he eventually came to the English king at York:

> he found the king all in confusion and no army mustered . . . Wherefore, when the said Earl of Carlisle perceived that the king of England neither knew how to rule his realm nor was able to defend it against the Scots, who year by year laid it more and more waste, he feared lest at last he [the king] should lose the entire kingdom; so he chose the less of two evils, and considered how much better it would be for the community of each realm if each king should possess his own kingdom freely and peacefully without homage, instead of so many homicides and arsons, captivities, plunderings and raidings taking place every year. (*Lanercost Chronicle*)

Harclay came to a secret agreement, a bond of mutual support, with Bruce at Bruce's castle of Lochmaben on 3 January 1323. Harclay, however, had local enemies and was surprised and arrested in Carlisle Castle. He was executed for treason on 2 March 1323. Edward II was not pleased to hear that a man recently made an earl should ally himself with an 'excommunicated enemy'.

Overleaf:
Byland Abbey. One of the great Cistercian monasteries in Yorkshire, Byland Abbey was established on this site in 1177. It was pillaged by the Scots in 1322.

A settlement between Edward II and Robert Bruce was in the offing, however. A thirteen-year truce was agreed at Bishopthorpe, near York on 30 May 1323. All attempts at negotiation had foundered previously on Edward II's refusal to recognise Bruce as king and to give up claims to sovereignty. Typically, Edward II's policy to Scotland (following that of his father) was more influenced by what was happening in France than in Scotland. The threat of war with France made him reconsider and agree a truce. Although this truce did not solve the fundamental differences of the two sides, it helped create an atmosphere conducive to reaching a solution. The years following 1323 saw an improvement in Robert Bruce's bargaining powers. In 1324, the Pope at last recognised Bruce as king. In this year, too, an heir to the throne was born, while in 1326 the Treaty of Corbeil renewed the alliance between Scotland and France, such a significant element in the Scottish war effort between 1296 and 1303. While Bruce's situation was strengthened both in Scotland and internationally, the position of Edward II deteriorated rapidly. The English King was deposed, probably on 20 January 1327, and succeeded by the young (fourteen-year-old) Edward III. It was an ideal time for Robert Bruce to assert his military power once more and it was probably not a coincidence that Edward III's coronation day, 1 February 1327, was chosen for a Scottish raid on Norham: 'The Scots . . . came in great force with ladders to Norham Castle which . . . had been very offensive to them. About sixteen of them boldly mounted the castle walls, but Robert de Maners, warden of the castle, had been warned of their coming by a certain Scot within the castle, and rushing suddenly upon them, killed nine or ten and took five of them alive, but severely wounded' (*Lanercost Chronicle*). The attack on Norham, in breach of the thirteen-year truce, was a reminder to the new regency government in England that the Scots were still pushing for the recognition that Robert Bruce sought and which they appeared to be getting closer to obtaining. The *Lanercost Chronicle* even reported that Edward II, on the eve of his deposition and desperate for support, wrote to the Scots 'freely giving up to them the land and realm of Scotland, to be held independently of any King of England, and [which was still worse] bestowed upon them with Scotland great part of the northern lands of England lying next to them, on condition that they should assist him against the queen, her son, and their confederates'.

Despite negotiations for peace, following the attack on Norham, both sides prepared for war. The Scots were the first to attack when fighting broke out again in the summer of 1327. Three columns led by James Douglas, Thomas Randolph, Earl of Moray, and Donald, Earl of Mar, attacked in the west through the Kielder Gap and the North Tyne. Robert Bruce was not involved in this attack. He was in Ulster in April 1327 where a power vacuum had emerged following the death, in 1326, of the Earl of Ulster. He had personal interests in the earldom, being husband of the previous earl's daughter, but was also making provision in Ireland for the coming war. It is in 1327 that reports of Robert Bruce's failing health arise from a number of sources. A letter from Ulster described Bruce as 'so feeble and so weak that he will not last much longer from this time, with the help of God, because he cannot move anything except his tongue'. The *Lanercost Chronicle* explained: 'My lord Robert de Brus, who had become leprous, did not invade England on this occasion'. The letter undoubtedly exaggerates Bruce's illness because the king did participate later in the Scottish campaigns in northern England. Barbour (*The Bruce*) described his illness in 1308: 'His strength failed him so completely that he could neither ride nor walk', and when it recurred in 1327, reported that 'the disease arose from catching a chill, for as a result of exposure when he was in great tribulations [1306–7] that serious illness came upon him'.

The encounter between English and Scottish armies in 1327 proved embarrassing for another English monarch. The young king marched north to Durham and tried, in vain, to bring the Scots to battle. The next strategy, to march north to Haydon Bridge on the Tyne in order to cut off their retreat to Scotland, proved counter-productive as they waited in vain as well as losing contact with the Scottish force. Having at last discovered that the Scots were in Stanhope Park (on the Wear), the king

Dunfermline Abbey tower. Edward I inflicted damage on Dunfermline Abbey, where he stayed in 1303. Robert Bruce helped to finance repair to the fire damage.

Whithorn Priory, Galloway. In the last few months of his life in 1329, Robert Bruce made a pilgrimage to the very popular St Ninian's shrine at Whithorn Priory.

Durham Castle. The castle was largely sheltered from Scottish raids by the bishop's policy of buying truces. In 1312 Bruce burnt the town 'scarcely attacking the castle'.

Dunstanburgh Castle, Northumberland. This castle was in a strange position for such a large stronghold as it guarded no strategic land or river route.

once more tried to engage the Scottish force. The Scots again evaded the English army but, in a night raid (4 August) led by James Douglas, the Scots attacked the English King's headquarters and almost captured him: 'Sir James of Douglas, like a brave and enterprising knight, stealthily penetrated far into the king's camp with a small party, and nearly reached the king's tent, but, in returning he made known who he was, killed many who were taken by surprise and escaped without a scratch.' To add to this near disaster – another attempt, in a string of such efforts since 1318, at capturing a major English hostage in order to force a peace on Scottish terms – the Scottish army 'silently decamped from the park, and marching round the King's army, held their way to Scotland'. Edward III 'shed tears of vexation, disbanded his army' and returned to York. Injury was added to English humiliation when the Scots, joined by Robert Bruce, harried the whole of Northumberland. Bruce himself besieged Norham Castle while James Douglas and Randolph, Earl of Moray, laid siege to Alnwick and Warkworth. This was a serious attempt to annex Northumberland, castles and land, to Scotland and it caused such concern that 'the people of the other English marches . . . sent envoys to the Scots, and for a large sum of money obtained from them a truce to last until [22 May 1328]'.

The English were, at last, forced into negotiations, talks starting in the autumn of 1327 and ending on 17 March 1328 with the Treaty of Edinburgh,

St Ninian's Cave, Whithorn. Veneration of the cave and St Ninian goes back to the eighth century when Galloway was under the influence of the Northumbrian kingdom.

Prudhoe Castle. Largely bypassed by the Scots, Prudhoe was in the hands of the Percies from the early fourteenth century. Much strengthening, for example of the barbican, occurred shortly afterwards.

Previous pages:
St Ninian's Cave, Whithorn.

ratified on the English side at Northampton on 4 May. Bruce's position as King of an independent Scotland was at last recognised; Edward III solemnly renounced all claims to English overlordship or sovereignty over Scotland; a marriage was contracted between Bruce's son and heir, David (aged four) and Edward's sister, Joan; and for his part, Bruce agreed to pay Edward III £20,000 for the sake of peace. This was a very large sum, roughly equivalent, according to some estimates, to the total amount taken by Scottish leaders in pacts for peace from the northern counties. To Bruce, now very ill and after so many attempts to force this recognition from England after 1314, it was a price worth paying. Acknowledgement by England itself was, however, not enough for Robert Bruce. To ensure international acceptance of his position, the Pope had to be persuaded to pledge the support Bruce required. Bruce wanted the Pope to put the final seal of approval on his kingship and sent envoys to ask him to grant the anointing and crowning of Scottish kings by the Bishop of St Andrews as the Pope's representative. Pope John XXII granted Bruce's request but, unfortunately, Bruce did not live to see the formal recognition of Scottish independence as the bull was issued on 13 June 1329, six days after his death at Cardross.

Melrose Abbey. Melrose's reputation as Scotland's premier monastic house was further enhanced by the burial of Robert Bruce's heart there.

A few years before his death, Bruce had a dwelling-house, not a castle, built at Cardross on the Clyde. It had a garden and a park for hunting.

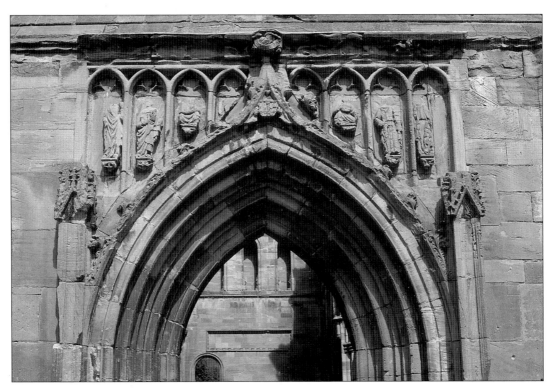

One of his last known journeys was a pilgrimage to the shrine of St Ninian at Whithorn in Galloway on 1 April 1329. He had, despite his many achievements, been unable to fulfil his ambition to fight on crusade and shortly before his death, he requested that his heart be taken on crusade by James Douglas.

The Treaty of Edinburgh/Northampton of 1328 was designed to be a 'true, final and perpetual peace between the kings, their heirs and successors and their realms and lands and their subjects and peoples'. In practice, the agreement only lasted four years but the achievements of Robert Bruce were more long-lasting. It has been seen that Bruce's role as leader of the Scottish nationalist cause was only part of his story. In many ways Robert Bruce's main achievement was to fulfil the aspirations of a very ambitious family. The family's territorial and dynastic ambitions started their long journey in north Yorkshire and south-west Scotland. In this context, Bannockburn in 1314 saw the confirmation of Robert Bruce's power in Scotland – Bruce had to be victor in a civil war before he could be a nationalist hero. Bruce's victory over his enemies in Scotland, the Comyns and their associates, is hardly as romantic as the notion of Bruce, saviour of Scottish nationhood, but it is, nevertheless, a most impressive achievement. Robert Bruce succeeded in stamping his authority over his Scottish rivals only between 1306 and 1314. His triumph over the Comyns, Macdougalls and the Earl of Ross, in northern Scotland, and the Balliols and Macdowells in the south-west, show that Bruce's war in Scotland was essentially a personal one aimed at control of areas subject to families who formed the political establishment in Scotland in 1286. Bannockburn confirmed the victories Bruce achieved against remarkable odds after 1307.

Scottish nationhood and Scottish identity were well established in Scotland before Robert Bruce asserted his political position in Scotland. The Declaration of Arbroath of 1320, that most famous statement of Scottish nationalism so inextricably linked with Robert Bruce, had several precedents. The Treaty of Birgham (1289) was a very clear expression of national identity by a Scottish government actively opposed by the Bruces since 1286. Nor, as has been seen, could Robert Bruce be set happily alongside William Wallace as comrades in arms for the nationalist cause. The Bruce 'nationalist' cause was the Bruce dynasty, and that this eventually became *the* nationalist cause is another remarkable story. Popular support in Scotland rallied to Robert Bruce because of his successes against the combined forces of the Comyns (and their associates) and their English allies. A civil war became a war of independence because Bruce had no option but to fight the English following his fatal wounding of John Comyn in 1306 and his usurpation of the Scottish crown shortly after. Popular reaction against Edward I's 'harsh' policies, strategic mistakes by Edward II in combating the Bruce 'coup' and Robert Bruce's skilful

Hadrian's Wall. Robert Bruce's Scottish raids on northern England resulted in a more systematic defence system in fourteenth-century Northumberland – the first since Roman times.

Etal Castle. This castle was licensed to fortify with battlements in 1341, common practice in fourteenth-century Northumberland.

military tactics ensured a Scottish morale strong enough to counter England's somewhat disorganised war effort.

The achievements of Robert Bruce have left a lasting impression on the Scottish psyche from the fourteenth century to the present day. What is sometimes understated, however, is the extent of Robert Bruce's impact and influence on people and places in his own day. Derided at first in a popular English story (told by Matthew of Westminster) as 'a summer king' whose kingdom would not last a year, Robert Bruce's influence ran strongly throughout Scotland, northern England and Ireland during his years of military triumph between 1307 and 1329. His military successes (and those of his allies) secured him control from the Highlands of Scotland to Berwick between 1307 and 1318; from Carlisle (Cumbria) to Beverley (East Yorkshire) between 1314 and 1322; from Ulster to Limerick in Ireland between 1315 and 1318. An examination of Robert Bruce's career shows the Bruces' development from a frontier family in northern England and south-west Scotland in the twelfth and thirteenth centuries to a family with their own 'Empire' between 1307 and 1329.

That was the reality of life for people in Scotland, northern England and (for a time) Ireland during these years.

Between 1307 and 1329, large towns in northern England, such as Carlisle, Durham, Newcastle and York, key areas of control, were put under immense pressure. Berwick had cracked but the major military bases, and all the castles of northern England, were reduced to impotent refuges for their neighbourhoods rather than active centres of resistance. Less well fortified institutions such as the many monasteries scattered across northen England were not as fortunate and suffered extensive economic loss, as did small towns and villages. Fear of loss of life, moveable goods and money was a reality in northen England in Robert Bruce's time. This 'fear' factor lived on beyond Robert Bruce's own lifetime. The legacy of Robert Bruce in England was the evolution of a truly military frontier zone that continued to be developed in fourteenth-century England – as far south as York but especially in the many stunning castles of Northumberland.

APPENDIX
ACCESS TO SITES

The sites listed below are manned and therefore subject to entry fees. All have the following standard opening times unless otherwise stated.

SUMMER: April–September, daily 9.30 a.m.–6.30 p.m.
WINTER: October–March, Monday–Saturday 9.30 a.m.–4.30 p.m., Sunday 2–4.30 p.m.

Caerlaverock Castle
Dirleton Castle
Melrose Abbey
Urquart Castle

WINTER: closed Thursday p.m. and all day Friday

Dunfermline Abbey
Sweetheart Abbey

WINTER: daily to 5 p.m. (not 4.30 p.m.)

Stirling Castle

WINTER: closed

Balvenie Castle
Dunstaffagne Castle
Kildrummy Castle

All other sites are unmanned and open at any reasonable time.

ENGLISH HERITAGE SITES

SUMMER: April–October, daily 10 a.m.–6 p.m.
WINTER: November–March, daily 10 a.m.–4 p.m.

Carlisle Castle
Clifford's Tower, York
Norham Castle
Richmond Castle
Rievaulx Abbey
Scarborough Castle
Warkworth Castle
Whitby Abbey

WINTER: Wednesday–Sunday only

Barnard Castle
Byland Abbey
Dunstanbrugh Castle
Furness Abbey
Middleham Castle

WINTER: closed

Etal Castle
Prudhoe Castle

BIBLIOGRAPHY

PRIMARY SOURCES (IN TRANSLATION)

Coss, P. (ed.). *Thomas Wright's Political Songs of England*, Cambridge University Press, 1996

Denholm-Young, N. (ed.). *Vita Edwardi Secundi*, London, 1957

Duncan, A.A.M. (ed.). *John Barbour's The Bruce*, Canongate, Edinburgh, 1997

King, E. (ed.). *William Hamilton of Gilbertfield's Blind Harry's Wallace*, Luath Press, Edinburgh, 1998

Maxwell, H. (tr.). *Chronicle of Lanercost 1272–1346*, James Maclehose and Sons, Glasgow, 1913

—— (tr.). *Scalacronica by Sir Thomas Gray*, James Maclehose and Sons, Glasgow, 1907

Skene, W.F. (ed.). *John of Fordun's Chronicle of the Scottish Nation*, The Historians of Scotland Vol IV, Edinburgh, 1872

Stones, E.L.G. (ed.). *Anglo-Scottish Relations 1174–1328: Some Selected Documents*, Clarendon Press, Oxford, 1963

Watt, D.E.R. (ed.). *Scotichronicon by Walter Bower*, Aberdeen, 1991

SECONDARY SOURCES

Barron, E.M. *The Scottish War of Independence*, Inverness, 1934

Barrow, G.W.S. *Scotland and its Neighbours in the Middle Ages*, Hambledon Press, London, 1992

——. *Robert Bruce*, Edinburgh University Press, 1988

——. *Feudal Britain*, Edward Arnold, London, 1956

Close-Brook, J. *Exploring Scotland's Heritage: the Highlands*, RCAHMS, Edinburgh, 1980

Cosgrave, A. (ed.). *A New History of Ireland: Medieval Ireland 1169–1534*, Oxford, 1987

Dalton, P. *Conquest, Anarchy and Lordship: Yorkshire 1066–1154*, Cambridge University Press, 1994

Duncan, A.A.M. *Scotland, the Making of the Kingdom*, Edinburgh University Press, 1992

Fisher, A. 'Wallace and Bruce', *History Today*, February 1989

——. *William Wallace*, John Donald, Edinburgh, 1986

Frame, R. *The Political Development of the British Isles, 1100–1400*, Oxford University Press, 1990

Grant, A. *Independence and Nationhood: Scotland 1306–1469*, Edward Arnold, London, 1984

Grant, A. and Stringer, K.J. (eds). *Medieval Scotland: Crown, Lordship and Community, Essays Presented to G.W.S. Barrow*, Edinburgh University Press, 1993, reprinted 1998

——. *Uniting the Kingdom: the Making of British History*, Routledge, London and New York, 1995

Lynch, M. *Scotland, A New History*, Pimlico, London, 1991

Macdonald, R.A. *The Kingdom of the Isles: Scotland's Western Seaboard*, Tuckwell Press, East Linton, 1997

MacNamee, C. *The Wars of the Bruces: Scotland, England and Ireland 1306–1328*, Tuckwell Press, East Linton, 1997

McNeil, P.G.B. and Macqueen, H.C. *Atlas of Scottish History to 1707*, The Scottish Medievalists and Department of Geography, University of Edinburgh, 1996

Prestwich, M. *Edward I*, Yale University Press, New Haven and London, 1988

——. 'England and Scotland During the Wars of Independence', *Scottish Historical Review* LXV (1986)

——. *York Civic Ordinances 1301*, Borthwick Papers 49 (University of York, 1976)

Reid, N. (ed.). *Scotland in the Reign of Alexander III 1249–1286*, Edinburgh, John Donald, 1990

Ritchie, G. and Harman, M. *Exploring Scotland's Heritage: Argyll and the Western Isles*, RCAHMS, Edinburgh, 1985

Shepherd, I.A.G. *Exploring Scotland's Heritage: Grampian*, RCAHMS, Edinburgh, 1986

Stell, G. *Exploring Scotland's Heritage: Dumfries and Galloway*, RCAHMS, Edinburgh, 1986

Stevenson, J.B. *Exploring Scotland's Heritage: the Clyde Estuary and Central Region*, RCAHMS, Edinburgh, 1985

Stringer, K.J. *Essays on the Nobility of Medieval Scotland*, John Donald, Edinburgh, 1985

Tabraham, C. *Scotland's Castles*, Batsford/Historic Scotland, London, 1997

Traquair, P. *Freedom's Sword: Scotland's War of Independence*, HarperCollins, London, 1998

Watson, F.J. *Under the Hammer: Edward I and Scotland 1286–1307*, Tuckwell Press, East Linton, 1998

Webster, B. *Medieval Scotland: the Making of an Identity*, MacMillan, London, 1997

Young, A. *Robert the Bruce's Rivals: the Comyns 1212–1314*, Tuckwell Press, East Linton, 1997, reprinted 1998

——. 'The North and Anglo-Scottish Relations in the Thirteenth Century', in J.C. Appleby and P. Dalton (eds), *Government, Society and Religion in Northern England 1000–1700*, Sutton Publishing, Stroud, 1997

——. 'The Bishopric of Durham in Stephen's Reign', in D. Rollason, M. Harvey and M. Prestwich, *Anglo-Norman Durham 1093–1193*, Boydell Press, Woodbridge, 1994, reprinted 1998

——. 'The Earls and Earldom of Buchan in the Thirteenth Century', in A. Grant and K.J. Stringer (eds), *Medieval Scotland: Crown, Lordship and Community*, Edinburgh University Press, 1993, reprinted 1998

——. 'Noble Families and Political Factions in the Reign of Alexander III', in N. Reid, *Scotland in the Reign of Alexander III 1249–86*, John Donald, Edinburgh, 1990

INDEX